Eyewitness Accounts of the American Revolution

The Journal of
Lt. William Feltman
1781-82

The New York Times & Arno Press

THE

JOURNAL

OF

LIEUT. WILLIAM FELTMAN,

OF THE FIRST PENNSYLVANIA REGIMENT,

1781–82.

INCLUDING

THE MARCH INTO VIRGINIA AND THE SIEGE OF YORKTOWN.

PHILADELPHIA:
PUBLISHED FOR THE HISTORICAL SOCIETY OF PENNSYLVANIA,
BY HENRY CAREY BAIRD
1853.

The Journal of Lieut. William Feltman, of the First Pennsylvania Regiment, from May 26, 1781 to April 25, 1782, embracing the Siege of Yorktown and the Southern Campaign.

[The Society is indebted to Horn R. Kneass, Esq., for permission to publish this Journal. The following letter from that gentleman to the Chairman of the Publishing Committee furnishes some particulars of the author.]

Dear Sir,—Lieut. William Feltman was a native of Lancaster County, Pennsylvania, which place he claimed as his residence as long as he lived.

He died a few years before the beginning of this century, but the precise year when he died, or his age at the time of his death, I am unable now to ascertain. The journal was handed to me over twenty years ago by my grand-mother, (now deceased,) who was a sister of Lieut. Feltman, and has been in my possession ever since.

Very respectfully yours,
HORN R. KNEASS.

Philadelphia, April 27, 1853.

York Town [Pennsylvania], 26*th May,* 1781. This day we left York at 9 o'clock in the morning with about eight hundred effective men, under the command of Gen. Wayne, and encamped 11 miles on the road to Frederick Town.

27*th.*—The general beat at sunrise, and we took up the line of march, and halted near Peter Little's Town—it being 14 miles.

28*th.*—The troops took up the line of march at sunrise, marched through Tarrey Town and halted near Pipe Creek, being about 14 miles.

29*th May.*—The troops took up the line of march at three o'clock in the morning, and encamped on the S. W. of Monococy—15 miles.

30*th.*—This day continued on the ground: the soldiers washed their clothing and furbished up their arms and accoutrements, and in the evening at 7 o'clock we were reviewed by Gen. Wayne.

31*st.*—Took up the line of march at sunrise; marched through Frederick Town, Maryland, where there was a number of British officers (prisoners), who took a view of us as we passed through the town. We made a very respectable appearance. We crossed the Pomock [Potomac] at Newland's ferry; were obliged to cross in bad scows. One unfortunately sunk, loaded with artillery, &c., and a few men, in which one Sergeant and three privates of our Regiment were drowned; encamped on this side of the river.

A number of us dined at the Tavern (or ornery as the Virginians call it.) The night turned out to be very heavy with rain, and we were obliged to take up our quarters in Col. Clapham's Negro Quarters, I mean a number of the officers of our Regiment. We rose early the next morning and breakfasted at said Ornery—18 miles.

June 1*st.*—Continued on our ground until 4 o'clock in the afternoon; moved 5 miles towards Leesburg, where I am informed that Dan'l May lives and keeps a public house. Loudon Co.—5 miles.

2*d.*—Continued on this ground till evening, it being very wet and disagreeable.

3*d.*—Took up the line of march at 10 o'clock A. M. Passed through

Leesburg, (which is but a very small town and not built regular.) We encamped at Goose Creek, being 15 miles.

4th.—Marched at six o'clock in the morning, and had orders from Gen. Wayne to leave our heavy baggage at this place (Mr. Corks's mills), and the sick of the line under the care of a surgeon. Marched through a low country, roads being very bad, in consequence of the rains we had a few days before, and encamped at the Red House, 18 miles—Prince William County.

5th.—A wet morning, cleared about 10 o'clock, A. M. Marched at 1 o'clock P. M., proceeded 12 miles towards Rappahannock, where we lay out without any kind of shelter—12 miles.

6th June.—March at six o'clock, A. M.—9 miles, Fauquier County.

7th.—Continued on our ground in consequence of a heavy rain.

8th.—Took up the line of march at sunrise. Reached the north branch of Rappahannock at 10 o'clock. The troops waded the river and proceeded 21 miles. Culpepper County.

9th.—Took up the line of march at six o'clock A. M., crossed the south branch of Rappahannock and proceeded 6 miles into the country. The country very poor and buildings very small—14 miles.

10th.—Took up the line of march at 5 o'clock in the morning—and joined the Marquis's troops this day, and passed a body of militia (Virginia) of 1800 men. We had a very severe march of 23 miles this day. (Orange Co.)

11th.—Marched at 4 o'clock and encamped at 10 A. M—10 miles.

12th.—Took up the line of march at 6 o'clock A. M.; march through a thicket of fine woods, nothing but a foot path, through which we got with a great difficulty, especially our artillery. At last we arrived on the main road leading to Fredericksburgh which I long wish for, and encamped 5 miles from where we entered on the road. (Louisa Co.)—14 miles.

13th.—Continued on this ground in order to refresh ourselves, which we had great occasion for.

14th.—Took up the line of march at 5 o'clock A. M.; marched through a d— poor county, the water being very scarce. This day see a number of Negroes, the greater part of them being naked—12 miles.

15th.—Took up the line of march at sunrise. A great scarcity of water that day and a very fatiguing march. Refreshed ourselves in an orchard with Col. Robinson. The Marquis and Gen. Wayne took a snack with us—14 miles. (Hanover County.)

16th June.—Took up the line of march at day break, made a short day's march of six miles, being much fatigued. This day built a fine bush hut—6 miles.

17th.—Took up the line of march at 3 o'clock in the morning, march through the best country we have ever seen in this State, and encamped at Mr. Dandridge's, being 20 miles.

18th.—Very fine morning. This day the enemy advanced on us. Our encampment struck at sunset. All the Continental Troops marched in order to surprise a party of Tarleton's horse. We continued till day light, but on our arrival found they had gone some hours—13 miles.

19th.—Lay on our arms till one o'clock; retired into the country 4 miles, where we lay destitute of any refreshment, bedding or covering— 4 miles, (Henrico Co.)

20th.—Marched at 6 o'clock, three miles, and were reviewed by the General. Lay on our arms all night—3 miles.

21st June.—Arrived at Col. Simm's mills. Marched at 12 o'clock A M., 8 miles, and lay at Burrill's ornery, destitute of every necessary of life—8 miles.

22d.—Marched at 2 o'clock through a well inhabited country, though I can give no account of the people, as I have not been in the inside of a house (but one or two ornerys). They sometimes come to the road side in order to take a view of us as we pass by, but a person can scarcely discern any part of them but the nose and eyes, as they have themselves muffled up with linens, &c., in order to prevent the sun from burning their faces (I mean the female sex). At the same time they will have a number of blacks standing around them, all naked, nothing to hide their nakedness. You can easily distinguish their sex; I mean the blacks, for reasons already mentioned. They will also have their attendants dressed in the same uniform. They will also attend their table in this manner.

*　　*　　*　　*　　*　　*　　*　　*　　*

This day we passed through Richmond in twenty hours after the enemy had evacuated it—a number of houses being destroyed by the enemy. They also destroyed a great quantity of Tobacco, which they threw into the streets and set fire to it. The town is built close on James River under a bank. We encamped two miles this side of the town. About 6 o'clock P. M. Capt. Davis and self made to town and spent the afternoon playing billiards and drinking wine—20 miles.

23d.—Took up the line of march at 2 o'clock in the morning, halted at 8 for refreshment, where we had an alarm. Our Light Horse brought us intelligence that the enemy was within one mile of us. The army immediately formed for action and an universal joy prevailed, that certain success was before us. We lay on our arms ten hours, hourly receiving accounts of their advance, (our intelligence on this whole march was exceeding bad), but to our great mortification it turned out a false alarm. At six we moved our position for convenience of encampment. A very heavy rain came on at 12 o'clock at night— 15 miles.

24th June.—Continued on this ground in order to dry our clothes (which had got wet the night before), and the men to furbish their arms, &c. This day one of our soldiers belonging to the fourth Reg't, Penna., was taken deserting to the enemy. At 3 o'clock P. M. he was tried and sentenced to be shot, which soon he received in the evening at roll-call. At the same time we received orders to strike our tents, which we did, and marched at dark in order to surprise Tarleton's Horse (12 miles.) He got intelligence of our advancing (which he always had, more than we) and retired—12 miles. James City County.

25th June.—Lay by this day. At dark took up our line of march in order to overtake Col. Simes's horse, who had the rear guard with a great number of cattle, plundering as he was making his way towards James Town; left one negro man with the small-pox lying on the road side in order to prevent the Virginia militia from pursuing them, which the enemy frequently did; left numbers in that condition starving and helpless, begging of us as we passed them for God's sake to kill them, as they were in great pain and misery.

26th June.—At six o'clock in the morning we were informed that a covering party of horse were but a small distance before us. Gen. Wayne immediately ordered the front platoon of each battalion to turn out immediately, which order being complied with, being four platoons and Major McPherson's party of Legionary horse, we pursued them five or six miles in full speed. At last we came within a short distance of them. Major Hamilton had the command of the Infantry. A party then of about forty men of the New England troops were ordered to mount behind the same number of dragoons, and then pursued them and came up with them in a short time. We had a severe skirmish with their Horse and Infantry, in which we took a number of their horse and cattle, and killed forty of their Infantry. Our loss was trifling. Major McPherson's horse threw him into the field of action, who fortunately made his escape. I expected every moment they would have attacked our small party of Infantry, which was posted on a small knoll, in order to cover the Light Dragoons.

27th June.—This day we lay at Bird's Ornery.

28th.—Made some movements for advantage of ground.

29th.—Manœuvred considerably in consequence of bad intelligence.

30th.—Greatly fatigued; lay by great part of this day. Our tents came to us this evening.

July 1st, '81—Marched at day break 8 miles to York River, for the troops to wash and refresh themselves, where one man and Dr. Downey of the 6th Reg't Penna. were unfortunately drowned. I mounted guard this day; returned that night to our former ground, I leaving the rear-guard of the army.

2d July.—Marched down to Bird's Ordinary, returned that night to our old encampment—8 miles.

3d.—Marched at sun [rise] to Mr.   Old Fields. Manœuvres retrograde and many, the troops almost worn out. Very hot weather.

4th.—A wet morning; cleared up 10 o'clock.

This day we had a Feu de Joie in celebration of our Independency of America. After that was over the Pennsylvania line performed several manœuvres, in which we fired; had the thanks of the Marquis. The feu de joie was with a running firing from right to left of the army.

5th.—Took up the line of march at 7 o'clock on our way to Williamsburg (which I should be very happy of seeing). Proceeded as far as Chickahomony Church, where we lay on our arms till sunrise—6 miles.

5th July.—At sunrise we took up the line of march for Jamestown, at which place the enemy lay encamped.

The first battalion of our line (the Pennsylvanians) was detached with a small party of riflemen, which brought on a scattering fire in front and on the flanks of our battalion (the first), that continued for two or three hours, between our Riflemen and their Yeagers; our battalion (the first) was then ordered to close column and advance, when we had information the 2nd and 3rd battalions with one of Infantry were in sight of us; we then formed again, displayed to the right and left, the 3rd battalion on our right and the 2nd on our left; being then formed, brought on a general engagement, our advance regular at a charge till we got within eighty yards of their whole army, they being regularly formed, standing one yard distance from each other, their Light Infantry being in front of our battalion. We advanced under a very heavy fire of grape-shot, at which distance we opened our musquetry. Then I received a wound with a canister shot in my left breast, but did not retreat until the whole of us retreated, which was very rapidly. Upon our retreat I felt very faintish, but the thoughts of falling into the enemy's hands made me push on as hard as I possibly could for about five miles, when I got a horse and rode to Bird's Ordinary, being 12 miles, where I arrived in the morning, 3 o'clock, my wound being very painful. List of the wounded officers of our line:

Capt. Cropley		Artillery		
Capt. Jirnney		6 Reg't Penna.		
do.	Doyle	do.	"	"
do.	Vanlear	5	"	"
do.	Stake	1	"	"
do.	McClelland	1	"	"
do.	Montgomery	4	"	"

Lieut Herbert wounded and taken and immediately paroled.

Lt. White	1st.
Lt. Piercy	2nd.

The number of our killed and wounded and taken being 97 Rank and File.

7th July.—This morning dressed my wound, which was very painful, but a very slight wound. In the afternoon went to see our wounded officers and soldiers at Bird's Ordinary.

Capt. Cropley's wound being very painful to him; likewise Lieut. Piercy's, both wounded through the thigh. Capts. Stake and McClelland slightly, through the calf of their legs.

8th.—Early this morning left Bird's Ordinary with our baggage, to join our troops, which then lay at Chickahomony Church. Marched three miles towards James River for camping.

9th.—Continued on the same ground for refreshment.

10th.—Marched at 1 o'clock P. M. to Holt's Iron Works; went a fishing to a small creek, where I see a cypress tree about 8 feet across the stump. Very elegant buildings, such as a grist and saw mill and a forge—14 miles.

11th.—Continued on the same ground in order for the men to wash and clean their linen and furbish their arms, &c. (Charles City County.)

12th.—Marched at 7 o'clock A. M. towards James River. Roads bad—14 miles.

13th.—Orders for cleaning ourselves and preparing for an incorporation, which was much wished for.

14th.—This day the Incorporation took place, when our officers knew who was for the Southern Campaign.

15th.—This day was taken up in crossing James River, when our supernumerary officers took their leave of us (where I saw the cane growing.)—8 miles.

16th July.—Marched at 3 o'clock in the morning for Chesterfield Court House; exceeding good water at this place. The ruins of a number of huts which the Virginians built for the use of their troops. An exceeding fine plain for the discipline and manœuvring of their troops—8 miles.

17th.—Marched at 3 o'clock in the morning and encamped at Chesterfield Court House—10 miles.

18th.—Marched at 3 o'clock P. M. to Cheatem's farm—12 miles.

19th.—Marched at 4 o'clock A. M. for Good's Bridge, where we arrived early this day—10 miles.

20th.—Continued this day.

21st.—Cloudy day.

22d.—This day a soldier of our regiment was hanged for marauding.

23d.—Paid Mr. Brooks a visit at his qnarters.

24th July.—Moved our encampment 200 yards in the rear. No particular account of the enemy.

25th.—About two o'clock this afternoon Good's Bridge fell into the creek. It was a great mercy there were no soldiers killed, as there were some under the bridge the time it fell.

26th.—Wet morning and a cloudy day.

27th.—A clear and fine morning.

28th.—Nothing material this day.

29th.—Ditto.

30th.—The general beat this morning at daybreak. The troops marched by the right to Watkin's Mill, where we arrived at 10 o'clock, A. M., being nine miles.

31st.—Lay still this day. The country here is the most fertile I have seen in this State, which is Amelia County.

August 1st.—Took up the line of march at daybreak—12 miles.

August 2d.—This day we marched to Namozin river—14 miles.

3d.—Marched to the right about for the north, (Dinwiddie County,)—21 miles.

4th.—Marched at daybreak for James River, opposite Westam—10 miles.

5th.—Crossed James River and took position on the heights of Westam—2 miles.

6th.—Remained on this ground this day, which place the enemy had occupied before us.

In the afternoon went a-fishing across James River; waded across, and was almost cast away, the water running very rapid. Caught no fish.

7th.—This day I went to see the curious works of Mr. Ballentine. He had made a canal about one mile along side of James River, which was about forty feet wide, in the centre of which was built a curious fish-basket. At the end of the canal was an elegant grist-mill with four pair of stones, close by which was the Bloomery or boring-mill, where they bored the cannon. Close by which was the Mansion House; four very large chimneys, built of the best brick I ever saw; each chimney has two air furnaces and a number of other works too tedious to mention. All those works were built at the expense of the State.

Within half a mile of these works is a very fine brewery.

All which elegant buildings were burnt by that d—d rascal,] Arnold. The brewery was saved by the intercession of the widow who owned part of it.

August 8th.—Marched at 1 o'clock in the morning, passed through Richmond at daylight, where I saw a number of Virginia and Maryland officers who were taken prisoners to the southward and paroled, and some exchanged, and encamped on our old ground two miles from Richmond—9 miles.

9th.—Took the line of march at one o'clock in the morning, and arrived at Savage's Farms, where we encamped near Bottom's Bridge, being 11 miles—New Kent County.

This day our heavy baggage arrived from Cock's Mill, which we long wished for. It being a very hot day, and little rain in the morning.

We once more came into a fine country, which we have not been for some time past.

10th.—Continued on this ground, it being very hot.

11th.—Continues a cloudy and rainy day. This day I see indigo growing.

August 12th.—This day a soldier of the Virginia Eighteen Months' Men was executed for entering the tent of Capt. Kirkpatrick, of 3d Regiment, and shooting him in the left eye.

This day I sent the following letters by Lieut. Crawford: One to Lieut. Johnson, one to Capt. Busk, of our Regiment, one to my mother, (No. 3,) one to my brother App. (No. 1.)

13th.—A little rain and very cloudy all day. The Marquis's troops crossed Pomonkey River. Evening and morning cool.

14th.—The day being very cool after yesterday's rain. Morning and evening cool.

15th.—This day being a very fine and clear day, Lieut. Milligan and self took a walk into the country for a few miles.

16th.—This day, about eight o'clock in the morning, Lieut. Crawford, of our Regiment, left the place bound for Pennsylvania, with a number of our soldiers' wives.

17th.—This morning, two o'clock, the general beat. The troops took up the line of march half an hour after, marched through a low country, more hilly than I have seen since we came to the State; encamped near Hanover Meeting-House, on Mr. George Philip's farm, one mile and a half from New Castle and four miles from Hanover Town, being 12 miles from Bottom's Bridge.

This morning our wounded officers left Hanover for Pennsylvania.

This evening I had an invitation from Capt. Pierson to assist him in eating two water-melons, which were the best and finest I ever see. This country is full of them; they have large patches of two and three acres of them.

The negroes here raise great quantities of snaps and collerds. They have no cabbage here. 12 miles.

August 18*th*.—This day Lieut. Collier and self took a walk to New Castle; spent the afternoon very agreeably in playing billiards, (which is a very bad one.) The town is situated on a very fine plain; there are but a small number of houses; the town is built very irregular; the town is covered all over with weeds. There are a few very elegant buildings. A few of us bucks remained in town all night at the ornery; got very merry.

August 19*th*.—This day we were reviewed by General Wayne. Our men made a very soldierly appearance; and from the parade we marched to a church close by our encampment, where Doct. Jones preached us a sermon.

20*th*.—A clear and fine day.

21*st*.—This day went a fishing, but caught no fish.

22*d*.—After having dined, a few of us, Lieut. Collier, &c., took a walk into the country about one and a half miles from our encampment, to one Mr. Chapman's, to eat water-melons, which we had in great plenty, with the addition of a little good spirits and water. His water and musk-melons were the best and finest that ever I saw either in Pennsylvania, Jersey, or any other place.

August 23*d*.—The troops took up the line of march at 9 o'clock in the morning for Bolton's Bridge, which we completed about one o'clock, P. M., and encamped at Mr. Savage's farms, being 10 miles.

24*th*.—The general beat this morning at 2 o'clock, the troops took up the line of march half an hour after; marched through Henrico county, past Mr. Randol Randolph's seat, which is a very elegant building, with the addition of a very large deer park, wherein is erected the deceased's monument.

Immediately after, we came into Charles City County, where we marched through the most level country that ever was seen, and encamped on Col. Byrd's farm close by his dwelling house, which is the most elegant building I ever saw.

All those buildings are built close on James river, which makes it appear heavenly.

He died a few years ago and was buried in his garden close by his house. A monument erected in the same place.

He was married to a Miss Willing from Philadelphia.

His neighbours are Col. Harrison, &c., where Gen. Wayne took up his quarters.

At four o'clock, P. M., I mounted the Advance Picquet Guard.

This day we marched a fatiguing march of twenty miles.

This place is called Westover—22 miles.

August 25*th*.—This morning I was relieved of picquet by Lieut. Ball. In the evening inspected.

26th.—Lieut. Collier and self went a fishing, and caught a fine parcel of yellow perch.

27th.—This day, 2 o'clock, P. M., a number of us crossed the James river in a canoe, in order to take a view of an elegant building and garden belonging to Colonel Mead. He very politely asked us in and gave us a drink of grog. In the evening Lieut. Collier and self went to Capt. Wilkins' tent, and there spent the evening and part of the night.

August 28th.—The troops took up the line of march at 9 o'clock, A. M., and encamped on Mauber hills near James river, and within half a mile of Mr. Randol Randolph's deer park—10 miles.

This day Captains Wilkin and Irvin of the Second Battalion were arrested by Col. Walton Stewart in consequence of our last night's proceedings.

29th.—This day I erected myself a very elegant berth, and promising myself comfortable sleeping for some time, but to my great mortification was disappointed. Gen. Muhlenberg's Aide de Camp came riding post haste into our camp about 11 o'clock, A. M. Our orders then immediately came for the troops to march at 2 o'clock, P. M. Lieut. Hammond and several other gentlemen, then embracing the opportutnity before we should march, immediately went to take a view of the monument which was erected in Mr. Randolph's deer park in memory of Richard Randolph and Jane his wife, (and also in memory of the deluge which happened in Virginia in the year 1771, which may be seen to endless ages.) Said Randolph has a very elegant seat.

The troops took up the line of march at 2 o'clock, P.M., and a very warm one it was, to be sure, and encamped at Westover, (the place we left yesterday,) being 10 miles.

August 30th.—This whole day was employed in crossing the troops and baggage over James river, and encamped on Col. Mead's farm.

This day, 2 o'clock, P. M., received the following letters, viz :

Two from my Brother, Michl. App. dated the 18th July, 81.

One from my Cousin Harry Dering, dated the 25th July, 81.

One from my friend Lieut. Thos. Doyle, dated blank.

The above mentioned letters I received from Lieut. Blewer of our line, who received them from a Virginia officer, who received them at Richmond.

This place is called Prince George County.

August 31st.—The general beat at half after one o'clock, P. M., and the troops took up the line of march at 2 o'clock, and encamped at Cabeen Island, being 12 miles   Surry county.

September 1st.—The troops took up the line of march at 9 o'clock this morning, and encamped at Surry Court House—12 miles.

This morning an express arrived in our camp, informing us that the French fleet was close by us, being 28 ships of the line, and 4 frigates ; all very large vessels, viz : One of 110 guns, three of eighty, ten of seventy-five, and all the rest sixty-fours—12 miles.

September 2d.—This morning at day-light, the troops took up the line of march and encamped opposite Jamestown, where lay a small English vessel under the sanction of a flag. We lay about two hours on our ground expecting every moment to see a glorious sight ; at last a number of large boats appeared in sight with about three thousand French troops on board, and also three large armed vessels to cover the troops landing.

The troops landed on our opposite side, on James's Island, and there encamped—which spread an universal joy amongst our officers and soldiers. Never did I behold a more beautiful and agreeable sight.

This morning I mounted the rear camp guard of our line.

This evening Gen. Wayne was unfortunately wounded in the thigh with a buck shot, by one of the Marquis's sentinels, which renders him unfit for duty—5 miles.

Sept. 3d.—This morning the general beat at 6 o'clock. The troops in half an hour after marched to James River, where the French boats lay in order to cross our troops. We landed below James's Island, and lay by the greatest part of the day, near the church, within half a mile of where we had the action of the 6th of July last. In the evening we marched for the Green Springs, and there lay that night without tent or any other shelter. A very heavy rain the whole time of our march.

Took a walk to take a view of the French troops, who make a very fine, soldierly appearance, they being all very tall men ; their uniform is white coats turned up with blue, their underclothes are white.

We left all our tents and baggage on the other side of the river.

This day three seventy-fours and one frigate went up York river, to block up the British vessels.

The Count de Grasse sent a flag to Lord Cornwallis, desiring him on his peril not to destroy any of his vessels, stores, &c.—2 miles.

Sept. 4th.—The troops took up the line of march at 4 o'clock this morning for Williamsburgh, (which is a place I long wished to see,) joined the Marquis la Fayette's corps of Infantry, about two miles from town—having no provisions this day nor yesterday, we formed our line close near the College, and were received by the French Gen. St. Simon, and a number of other French gentry. In the evening our troops quartered in the College—7 miles.

Sept. 5th.—This day marched back again one mile in order for our men to wash their clothing and cook provisions.

Took a walk to town with a number of our gentlemen, and took a view of the town, as it is the metropolis of Virginia. There are some very elegant buildings, such as the College, Palace, Capitol or State House, in which is erected a statue of marble, the image of Lieut. Gen. Berkely, Governor of the State of Virginia, &c.

As we passed through town Doct. Nicholson very politely asked as to walk with him to his house ; we were very elegantly entertained with a good dinner, a glass of good spirits and Maderia wine.

Sept. 6th.—This morning 8 o'clock, the troops took up a line of march and marched through Williamsburg towards Yorktown, and encamped near Col. Nat. Burrell's mill, which is a very advantageous post.

At said Mr. Burrell's mill I had the pleasure of seeing rice growing, which I thought was a great curiosity. It grows about two feet high, with one long small leaf and exactly like the top or seed of Indian corn. It grows in low marshy ground—4 miles.

7th.—This morning I mounted the rear picquet of our line. As we were on the grand parade, a party of the enemy's Dragoons drove a party of our Horse within our advance picquet, where they were very warmly received by them with a platoon of musketry; they immediately retired. All our guards marched to Mr. Burrell's mills, and there took post, where we remained for some time expecting them to return again. We were then ordered to march to our respective post.

In the evening I marched my picquet within one mile and a half York river.

Sept. 8th.—The troops took up the line of march this morning at 9 o'clock, marched through Williamsburgh, and encamped half a mile from town with the French army and Light Infantry—4 miles.

9th.—This day our baggage came up. At 5 o'clock this evening, the Light Infantry and our troops were received by the Marquis la Fayette and the French General, St. Simon, and a number of other gentlemen.

Sept 10th.—This day the enemy took two of our Dragoons prisoners, and we took five of theirs.

11th.—This day I walked with a number of French gentlemen (of the Huzzars) at their request. The Baron Deweck, an elderly gentleman, being a German, so that he and I were very sociable. We dined at the widow Crings', where we had an elegant dinner, but nothing to drink but small beer.

12th.—This day a number of our gentlemen officers were introduced to the French General, St. Simon.

In the afternoon reviewed by ditto.

Sept. 13th.—About one or two o'clock this morning, we had the heaviest clap of thunder (remarked) ever heard. Also a very heavy rain all that night.

This day Gen. Wayne and the Baron Steuben dined with our field officers.

14th.—This day I mounted the Centre Picquet near the Windmill, in Williamsburg. In the evening about four o'clock twenty-one pieces of cannon were fired on the arrival of his Excellency, General George Washington.

There was a universal joy amongst our officers and soldiers, especially the French troops, on his arrival.

This night about twelve o'clock a French officer came to my picquet and desired me to send a file of men with him, to the Marquis La Fayette's quarters, as he had a packet of letters for him from the Count De Grasse. He informed me (as he spoke German) there were nine large men of war joined the Count De Grasse the day before yesterday from Rhode Island under the command of Count Rochambeau.

He likewise informed me that the day before yesterday they took two of the enemy's frigates of thirty two guns each. Also, the last vessels had a reinforcement of two thousand five hundred French Infantry on board.

I had about one hour's confab with the gentleman, and he seemed much pleased with our present situation, and was very desirous of explaining himself in a more explicit manner, as he spoke but very indifferently the German language. He was confident that Lord Cornwallis would not stand it longer than eight days at farthest.

Sept'r 15*th.*—This morning about two o'clock, as I was walking up and down past one of my sentinels in order to keep myself awake, I was very agreeably entertained by the singing of a mocking-bird. He sang by himself and continued his notes till day-light. One would have imagined that he was sensible of the merit of his accomplishments and that it was in complaisance to man as well as for his satisfaction that he was pleased to sing when all was silent (but the barking of some —— dogs). Nothing animated him so much as the stillness of nature; 'twas then that he composed and executed all his tones. He raised from seriousness to gaiety, and from a simple song to a more sportive warbling, from the lightest quivers and divisions, he softened into the most languishing and plaintive sighs, which he afterwards forsook to return to his natural sprightliness.

Interrupted by the passing and repassing of the soldiers, waggons, &c. by examining them.

This day we had a very heavy shower of rain.

16*th Sept'r.*—This afternoon at 2 o'clock I had the pleasure of being introduced to his excellency Gen. Geo. Washington, Esq., Commander-in-Chief of all the American and French forces now in America.

17*th Sep'tr.*—This morning went to College Landing, crabbing; we caught three dozen. We also had a great deal of diversion in catching them. In the afternoon heavy rain and continued until night.

18*th.*—This being a very fine day and nothing to do, went a crabbing.

19*th.*—This being a very excesssive warm day as we have had this summer—found out a new billiard table in Williamsburgh but not a very good one.

20*th Sept'r.*—This morning I mounted the picquet at College Landing. A very great change of weather this day, it being dull and very cold and unwholesome day. Rained very hard all night.

This evening received a letter from my friend Lieut. James McLean dated at Philad'a, July 22d, 1781.

21*st Sept'r.*—This being a very cold day, bought our corn for three pounds, Virginian money.

22*d.*—This day the Northern troops arrived and landed at Burrell's Landing.

This morning received a letter from Lieut. Andrew Johnston from York (Penna.) dated the 3d Sept'r, 1781.

After breakfast Lieut. Benj'n Lodge and self took a walk to Lieuts. Ball and Armstrong's quarters; spent the day very agreeably with them in playing whilst, fowling, &c.

23*d Sept'r.*—This day eleven o'clock A. M., I had the pleasure with a number of other gentlemen officers to be introduced to the Count Rochambeau at the Marquis's quarters. He is an elderly gentleman, of

15

about five feet six inches high, and has a very soldierly appearance; is a man well experienced of war, &c.

24*th* *Sept'r*.—This morning I wrote the following letters, viz.

One to my brother App. No. 8; one to Lieut. Johnston, No. 2, and one [to] cousin Harry Dering, No. 1.

The above letters I sent by a soldier, Wm. Noble, who got his discharge from the 4th Reg't, Penna.

25*th* *Sept'r*, '81.—Spent this day at the billiard table in town, and in the evening went to a hop.

26*th*.—This day Lieut. Striker, 6 others and self took a ride to Col. Toliver's,* where Lieut. Wm. Moore lay sick with the fever and ague; dined very sumptuously and spent the afternoon with him; said Toliver has a very elegant seat about three miles from Williamsburgh.

27*th*.—This morning half past seven o'clock the general beat, and at eight o'clock the Infantry and our Brigade took up the line of march and encamped half a mile this side of Williamsburgh along with the rest of the army.

28*th*.—The whole army took up the line of march this morning five o'clock. I conjecture the whole of our army, I mean the French and our Continental troops, to be Fifteen Thousand Veteran Troops, besides the militia; they are so numerous that I have not been able to ascertain their number. The American army consists of six Brigades, viz: Col. Vons's, Lt. Col. Barber's and Lt. Col. Gemot's Battalion of Infantry will form one brigade and to be commanded by Brigadier Gen. Muhlenberg.

Col. Scammell's Reg't and Lt. Col. Hamilton's Battalion of Infantry and Harem's Reg't, a Brigade to be commanded by Brigadier Gen. Harem.

Col. Gaskin's Virginia Reg't and the two Battalions of Pennsylvania's, a Brigade to be commanded by Brigad'r Gen. Wayne.

The two Jersey battalions and the Rhode Island Reg't, a Brigade to be commanded by Col. Dayton.

The third and fourth Maryland Regt's, a Brigade to be commanded by Brigad'r Gen'l Clinton.

The American troops encamped in a wood within a mile of the Enemy's left line—and the French troops encamped on their right. Our troops remained under arms all night with their respective companies and platoons.

The French troops saluted Col. Tarleton's Horse with a few shot of three pounders which made them retreat immediately.

A number of prisoners taken this night who had been straggling through the country.

29*th*.—This morning 7 o'clock the army took up the line of march, and formed in front of a morass and in front of the enemy's works, being about half a mile from their outworks.

The two Brigades of Infantry crossed the morass, who were immediately saluted with a few cannon shot. One of their soldiers unfortunately lost his leg by a cannon ball.

* Taliaferro is thus pronounced.

3

A nine pound and a three pound shot paid us a visit in camp, but [we] received no damage from them.

30*th Sept'r.*—This morning about 8 o'clock, upon strict examination, we found that the enemy had evacuated all their outworks, which we immediately took possession of. The French and British had a severe engagement this morning. One of the French officers lost his leg, and a number of the privates killed and wounded.

Col. Scammell was wounded and taken prisoner this morning.

Lt. Tilden and self took a walk to view their works which they evacuated last night, which was within musket shot of their main works, when we perceived a flag advancing towards us, which we immediately went to meet, and on examination found that he had a letter for Lieut. Col. Huntington of Col. Scammel's Reg't, informing him of his captivity, and desiring him to send his waiter and clothing to Williamsburgh, where he would be sent on parole as soon as his wound was dressed.

This day Capt. Davis laid a bet with me of a beaver hat that Lord Cornwallis and his army would be prisoners of war by the next Sunday.

This evening Capt. Smith of our battalion, a sub. from Col. Gaskin's Reg't, and self, with fifty men, mounted the advance guard in front of the enemy's left, near the ruins of a mill.

1*st Oct'r.*—This morning the enemy discharged a number of their horses, which were so poor that they were scarcely able to walk.

This afternoon, three o'clock, his excellency Gen'l Washington, Gen. Duportail and several other engineers crossed at the mill dam to take a view of the enemy's works. His excellency sent one of his Aides de Camp for Capt. Smith and his guard of fifty men to march in front of his Excellency as a covering party, which we did, and went under cover of a hill, where we posted our guard, when his Excellency Gen'l Washington and Gen'l Duportail with three men of our guard advanced within three hundred yards of the enemy's main works, which is the town of York.

Capt. Smith, and Lt. Parker and self took a walk to the York River, where we had the pleasure of seeing all the enemy s vessels, of which they had four of them sunk this side of the river in order to prevent the French shipping from passing this side. We observed at a great distance down the river three of the French ships riding at anchor.

The enemy this whole day keep up a cannonading at our fatigue parties who were throwing up works in front of them at so short a distance as half a mile, but did very little damage.

We waited this whole day very impatiently, but all to no purpose, in expectation of being relieved from picquet, but to our great mortification we found that we were to be continued, which we very agreeably consented to, and built ourselves a fine bowery of pine bushes to spend the night and to keep the dew from us.

2*d Oct'r.*—A continual cannonading this whole day at our fatigue parties. One Maryland soldier's hand shot off and one militia man killed.

One of the Maryland soldiers deserted to the enemy this afternoon from his post; my waiter was in pursuit of him, but could not overtake him, and in his pursuing him made him drop his arms and accoutrements, which he brought off with him.

Four of the enemy's Dragoon horses made their escape from them this day and were taken up by our riflemen.

This evening 6 o'clock our picquet was ordered to return to camp.

This day received the following letters, viz:

One from Lt. Johnston dated York Town (no date) with three newspapers enclosed.

One from Lt. White dated York, 9th Sept'r. 1781.

One from Lt. Everly at York Town, Sept'r. 10th, 1781.

3d Oct'r.—Very little firing this whole day. Last night three men of Capt. Rice's comp'y were killed at our works with a cannon ball and one badly wounded, all with one shot.

4th.—Last night four hundred men of our Brigade went on fatigue. Very little firing this day. A number of heavy pieces of artillery arrived in camp this day. This afternoon Capt. Steel and self paid a visit to Capt. John Irwin formerly of 2nd Reg't, but now in the staff department. We dined with him and spent the afternoon drinking a sup of good grog.

This day two of the British deserted to us soldiers.

5th Oct'r, '81.—This morning a very heavy cannonading and firing with musquetry. Our patroles meeting with each other caused the firing.

This day our Battalion was ordered on picquet at the Redoubt No. 1, where a Corporal of Capt. Bond's company was shot through the rump with a nine-pounder as he was relieving the sentinels. He was immediately brought into the fort and the Doctor sent for, who informed us that his life was but short. The Doctor then ordered him to be carried to camp, where he lived but a short time.

In the evening we were relieved by Col. Duey, commanding the Rhode Island Reg't.

6th Oct'r, '81.—This morning six o'clock our two Penna. Reg'ts, the two Reg'ts of Maryland and a number of militia were ordered each man to make a gabion, which we did before twelve o'clock, M. Very little firing done this day.

7th.—All last night a very heavy cannonading, and this morning, at the French troops, two of their men killed. Last evening about three thousand of the French and our troops with their arms, &c. went to break ground. This morning Capt. Steel, Lieut. Ball and self took a walk to see what work was done. We found to our great satisfaction that they had a parallel line from the bank of the river extending beyond the redoubt No. 2, with the addition of two small batteries, &c.

This day received the following letters, viz:

One from my Brother App dated Lancaster, Sept'r, 10th, 81, No. 3, but received but two, and one from Lt. Andrew Johnston dated York Town, Sept'r 11th, 1781, with a number of newspapers inclosed.

This day I won a beaver hat from Capt. Davis.

8th Oct'r.—This day I bet a pair of silk stockings with Capt. Davis that Cornwallis and his army would not be prisoners of war by this day two weeks.

This afternoon our Division went on fatigue to forward our works near the enemy's lines. They keep up a continual firing this whole day.

This afternoon a French officer got his leg shot off by a cannon ball from the British; he was advanced in front of our works.

9th Oct'r.—Last night one of Capt. Bartholomew's men was killed with a cannon ball on our works.

This morning we completed a very elegant battery for ten pieces of heavy artillery, viz: Three twenty four pounders, three eighteen pounders, two eight-inch howitzers, two ten and a half inch mortars fixed upon carriages (and not upon beds) in order to throw the shot horizontal into the enemy's works, and there to burst and destroy their works. We have six of those mortars; they were invented by Gen. Knox and proved to be of effect.

This morning 9 o'clock A. M. a deserter from the enemy's artillery came to us; he left them just as their piece fired, which was advanced in front of the Governor's House. He informed us that Cornwallis had given out orders to them not to be afraid of the Americans, that they had not any heavy pieces of ordinance except a few pieces of field artillery. He also informed the soldiery and inhabitants that the French fleet was inferior to him and were afraid to attack him; that they came to this place to procure a quantity of tobacco, and if they could not be supplied here, that the fleet would set sail in eight or ten days at the farthest, and leave the continent. Such are my Lord's addresses to his soldiery, but they have more sense than to believe his weak expressions.

This day 12 o'clock M. we were relieved by Gen. Clinton's Division.

This afternoon four o'clock our Division was ordered on Fatigue, after four and twenty hours' very hard working at our lines, &c.

In the evening we opened our battery of ten pieces upon the right of our works, and gave the British a few heavy shots and a number of ten and a half inch shells, &c.

The French at the same time opened their batteries upon them.

10th Oct'r.—This whole day a very heavy cannonading on both sides.

This afternoon our whole Division was turned out for fatigue for to make fascines, gabions, saucissons, palisades, pickets, &c. and had them carried to the front of our respective regiments.

This day wrote a letter to Lt. Johnston at York Town, Penna. and sent it by a soldier of our Battalion.

11th Oct'r, '81.—Last night about seven o'clock I was taking a view of the shells we threw into York, which was very pleasing to see, and shortly after I perceived a large thick black smoke rising which I conjectured was the enemy's burning some of their vessels, but after inquiring into the matter found they were set on fire by some of our shells which were thrown among their shipping accidentally. This morning another of their vessels was burnt.

This day eleven o'clock our whole Division went on fatigue on the lines.

This whole day we cannonaded the enemy, and sent them a number of shells, and drove their artillery from the embrasures, and they had not the spirit to return one shot this whole day.

Head Quarters before York, Oct'r 11th, 1781.

At a General Court Martial of the line held at camp before York Oct'r 2d, and continued by adjournments, whereof Col. Dayton was President, Capt. P. Duffy of the Fourth Regiment of Artillery charged with scandalous and infamous behaviour unbecoming the character of an officer and gentleman on the night of the 23d and morning of the 24th Sept'r last, such as drawing a sword on Capt. Ballard and attempting to stab him, and firing a pistol at him when unarmed, also for a most disgraceful breach of friendship in seizing from Lt. Blewer a loaded pistol and snapping the same at him, when attempting, at Capt. Duffy's own request, an amicable settlement of his (Capt. Duffy's) quarrel with Capt. Ballard; also charged by Lt. Col. John Stewart, *first*, with being drunk; *2d*, rioting in the street; *3d*, abusing a French soldier; *4th*, Violation of good discipline in having in a seditious and disorderly [manner] threatened a French guard stationed at the Hospital for the security of the sick—was tried. The Court, after mature deliberation, are of opinion that Capt. Duffy drew a sword on Capt. Ballard and attempted to stab him when unarmed on the evening of the 23d Sept'r last, and on the morning of the 24th drew his sword on Capt. Ballard, he having one by his side; that Capt. Duffy also seized a pistol from Lt. Blewer and snapped it at him, on the before mentioned evening, declaring he would shoot him, when Lt. Blewer was attempting at Capt. Duffy's own request an amicable settlement of his quarrel with Capt. Ballard. It does not appear to the Court that the pistol Capt. Duffy seized from Lt. Blewer was loaded. The Court are of opinion that Capt. Duffy's conduct, as found, is a breach of Article 21st, section 24th, of the Rules and Articles of War—and sentence him to be discharged the service.

The Commander-in-Chief approved the foregoing sentence.

12th Oct'r, '81.—Last evening at 5 o'clock, a Detachment from our Division was ordered on fatigue, in order to run the second parallel, where I had the honour to be one of the number, and had a command of eighty two men and another officer with me. Every second man of the whole detachment carried a fascine and shovel or a spade, and every man a shovel, spade or grubbing hoe.

Just at dusk we advanced within gun-shot of the enemy, then began our work. In one hour's time we had ourselves completely covered, so we disregarded their cannonading; they discharged a number of pieces at our party, but they had but little effect, they only wounded one of our men. We were in the center of two fires, from the enemy and our own, but the latter was very dangerous; we had two men killed and one badly wounded from the French batteries, also a number of shells bursted in the air above our heads, which was very dangerous to us. We dug the ditch three and a half feet deep and seven feet in width In the morning before daylight we were relieved by the militia.

This morning two Hessian deserters came to us.

This morning the enemy threw a number of shells amongst the militia who were at work on the second parallel line.

This day 12 o'clock we were relieved by Gen. Lincoln's Division, when our division marched off with drums beating and colours flying. This day I being very much fatigued.

This afternoon a fatigue party was ordered from our Division to cut palisades.

This day a very heavy cannonading both from the enemy and our side, also a great number of shells thrown.

13th Oct'r, '81.—This morning our whole Division went on fatigue; making saucissons, fascines, gabions, pickets, &c. for the use of our batteries. We completed our task before 12 o'clock M.

This whole day cannonading from both sides.

This afternoon Col. Moylan's Horse, &c. marched to the southward.

14th Oct'r.—Last night a very heavy cannonading.

This morning 10 o'clock our Division mounted in trenches; this day we had a number of our men killed and wounded. Capt. Steel had one of his company very badly wounded. The enemy this whole day keep up a continual firing of cannon and throwing a number of five inch shells. The latter are very dangerous, especially in the day-time, as they cannot be perceived only [except] by a little noise they make as they fall.

This whole day our men were carrying gabions, fascines, &c. . This evening it is reported there is something grand to be done by our Infantry.

15th Oct'r, '81.—Last evening, just at dusk, two of our Regiments of Light Infantry, under the command of the Marquis La Fayette, came to the trenches. Immediately after, they advanced towards the enemy's two out-works, which they stormed and carried with success with the loss of a few killed and wounded. The following officers were wounded, viz: Col. Barber, Major Barber, Capt. Ohlney and a few volunteers; the number of men cannot be yet ascertained. The French carried one work and our Infantry another; both parties behaved with great spirit. The French had likewise a number of killed and wounded.

In those two redoubts were taken the following officers, viz : One Major, two Captains, two Lieutenants and one Ensign, and the number of Privates not yet known.

The French and our Infantry killed a number of the enemy in the storm.

When the Light Infantry advanced, the one-half of our Division were ordered on fatigue to complete our Second Parallel line ; each man of the fatigue party carried a fascine, a shovel or a spade ; and the remainder of our Division went as a Covering party to our troops who stormed the works. We were very much exposed to the enemy's fire, both musquetry and cannon balls and grape shot, and not a single man hurt.

This day we completed our Second Parallel line.

The enemy threw a number of shells this day and wounded a great number of men, especially the militia; several were wounded this day in their sleep, such is the carelessness of those stupid wretches who are not acquainted with the life of a soldier.

This morning his Excellency Genl. Washington sent a flag to Lord Cornwallis, but what the contents were I could not learn.

This day 12 o'clock our troops were relieved by Genl. Lincoln's Division, when we march off with drums beating and colours flying, after a very fatiguing night.

Our Second Parallel line is now within two hundred- and fifty yards of the enemy's main works, which is York Town ; where we have a very fine prospect of Town, River and the enemy's shipping, also of the town of Gloster, which is on the opposite shore.

Upon the right of our line we are erecting a twelve-gun battery.

This whole day being very quiet, very little firing on either side, only throwing a few shells.

16th Oct. '81.—This morning at daylight the enemy sallied out, but with what force we cannot learn. They took possession of one of our batteries and spiked a few of our cannon with their bayonets. Our troops immediately attacked them and drove them to town with a considerable loss. Eight of them were found dead on the spot with a number of wounded.

This day 11 o'clock A. M. our Division went on fatigue, making saucissons, fascines, gabions, &c.

17th Oct'r.—This day 11 o'clock A. M. our Division mounted the trenches. A few shells thrown by the enemy.

This day flags passing and repassing. Lord Cornwallis proposed deputies from each army to meet at Moore's House to agree on terms for the surrender of the garrison at York and Gloster, and hostilities to cease for twenty-four hours. His Excellency Genl. Washington allowed my Lord but two hours. An answer was sent at 3 o'clock P. M. when a cessation of arms took place.

Lord Cornwallis sent a flag ; he would surrender himself prisoner of war, only allowing him some small preliminaries which would be settled in the morning.

This day we finished a very fine battery of fifteen pieces of heavy ordinance.

18th Oct'r.—Flags passing and repassing this whole day. This day our fleet hove in sight with a detachment from Penna.

This afternoon Lieuts. Martin, V. Henley and self took a walk to the left of our lines, where we found the following batteries all ready to be opened at one moment's time, viz :

No. 1. From the right. One iron 18 pounder, 2 Howitzers, 2 Mortars and 2 Royals.

No. 2. Ten 18 pounders, &c., three Ten-Inch Mortars, one Eight-Inch Howitzer, two Royals.

No. 3. Two 10 Inch Mortars and 2 Royals.

No. 4. Four 18 pounders, iron pieces.

No. 5. Four 18 pounders and 2 Twenty-fours. (All Brass.)

No. 6.   Do.   Do.

No. 7. Six Twenty-four Pounders (all brass.)

No. 8. One Eight Inch Howitzer ; Eight Thirteen Inch Mortars and 2 Royals (all brass.)

We could not pass the ravine to see the remainder of our work.

19th Oct'r. '81.—At one o'clock this day Major Hamilton with a detachment marched into town and took possession of the batteries and hoisted the American flag.

The British army marched out and grounded their arms in front of our line. Our whole army drew up for them to march through, the French army on their right and the American army on their left.

The British prisoners all appeared to be much in liquor.

After they grounded their arms they returned to town again.

20th Oct'r.—This day the prisoners remained in town.

Lt. Collins and self took a walk to see our gentlemen officers who had just landed, and took a sup of grog with them.

Head Quarters near York, October 20th, 1781.

The General congratulates the army upon the glorious event of yesterday. The generous proofs which his Most Christian Majesty has given of his attachment to the cause of America must force conviction in the minds of the most deceived among the enemy, relatively to the decisive good consequences of the alliance, and inspire every citizen of these States with sentiments of the most unutterable gratitude. His fleet, the most numerous and powerful that ever appeared in these seas, commanded by an Admiral whose fortune and talents insure great events; an army of the most admirable composition, both in officers and men, are the pledges of his friendship to the United States, and their co-operation has secured us the present signal success.

The Genl. upon this occasion intreats his Excellency Count De Rochambeau to accept of his most grateful acknowledgments for his councils and assistance at all times. He presents his warmest thanks to the General Baron De Viominel, Chevalier Chastellux, Marquis De St. Simon and Count De Viominel, and to Brigadier Genl. De Choisey (who had a separate command) for the illustrious manner in which they have advanced the interest of the common cause.

He requests the Count De Rochambeau will be pleased to communicate to the army under his immediate command the high sense he entertains of the distinguished merits of the officers and soldiers of every corps, and that he will present in his name to the regiment of Agenors and Deuxponts the pieces of brass ordinance captured by them, as a testimony for their gallantry in storming the enemy's redoubts on the night of the fourteenth instant, when officers and men so universally vied with each other in the exercise of every soldierly virtue.

The General's thanks to each individual of merit would comprehend the whole army, but he thinks himself bound by affection, duty and gratitude to express his obligations to Major Generals Lincoln, La Fayette and Steuben, for their disposition in the trenches; to Gen. Du Portail and Col. Carney for their vigour and knowledge which were conspicuous in their conduct of the attacks; and to Gen. Knox and Col. De Abbervaille for their great care, attention and fatigue in bringing forward the artillery and stores, and for their judicious and spirited management of them in the parallels. He requests the gentlemen above mentioned to communicate his thanks to the officers and soldiers of their respective commands.

Ingratitude, which the General hopes never to be guilty of, would be conspicuous in him, was he to omit thanking in the warmest terms his Excellency Governor Wilson, for the aid he has received from him and from the militia under his command, to whose activity, emulation and courage such applause is due. The greatness of the acquisition would be an ample compensation for the hardships and hazards which they encountered with so much patriotism and firmness.

In order to diffuse the general joy in every breast, the Genl. orders [that] those men belonging to the army who may now be in confinement shall be pardoned, released and join their respective corps.

Divine service is to be performed in the several Brigades or Divisions. The Commander in Chief earnestly recommends it that the troops not on duty should universally attend, with that seriousness of deportment and gratitude of heart which the recognition of such reiterated and astonishing interpositions of Providence demands of us.

21st. Oct'r. '81.—This afternoon the prisoners marched out of town, under the care of three Divisions of militia.

This day Lt. Thomas Doyle and self took a walk to town, where we found all the houses ruined and destroyed.

In this day's Gen'l. Orders, the troops are to be in readiness to move at the shortest notice.

Division Orders of this day.

The Baron Steuben feels himself particularly happy in complying with the request of his Excellency Genl. Washington in presenting his warmest thanks to the officers and soldiers of his Division, for the great skill and alacrity with which they performed the several duties assigned them during the siege against York. He ever entertained the highest opinion of the troops, but the spirit and bravery which was so conspicuous on the present occasion has given him additional confidence in them and secured his warmest and lasting friendship.

He cannot be too thankful to Brigadier Genls. Wayne and Gist for their gallant behaviour on all occasions, and the great assistance they afforded him during the whole of the operations. He also wishes Col. Butler, Col. Stewart, Major Hamilton, Major Willis, Major Edwards and Major Roxburgh, the officers and soldiers under their command, to accept his best thanks for the good conduct shewn in opening the second parallel, which he considers as the most important part of the siege. He takes pleasure in assuring them it was performed with a degree of bravery and dispatch that exceeded his most sanguine expectations.

He cannot conclude without expressing in the highest terms his approbation respecting the conduct of Captain Walker, who performed double duty in the trenches, by mounting with his company, in addition to the services he rendered him as his Aide de Camp, which was so great as to entitle him to his sincere acknowledgments.

This day received the following letters, viz:

One from my brother Frederick Kneass, dated the 10th Oct'r. 81.
One from my brother App, dated the 10th Oct'r. 81.
One from Lt. Johnston, dated York Town, Oct'r. 12, 81.
One from some person or other [who] signed himself Incognito.

22d *Oct'r.* '81.—This morning I wrote the following letters, viz: One to my mother, and one to my brother App. No. 9.

This morning our brigade went on duty to York and Gloster.

23d *Oct'r.*—This morning Capt. Stevenson and self crossed the river to take a view of Gloster, which we found full of sick of the British.

This afternoon Col. Tarlton was dismounted from his horse by an inhabitant who owned the horse.

Spent the afternoon very agreeably drinking wine and claret, &c.

24th.—The French troops are employed this day in taking their heavy pieces of ordinance.

This day wrote a letter to my Brother App., No. 10.

Spent the afternoon with the Officers of the Third Penn'a Battalion.

Return of the Garrison of York and Gloucester, in Virginia, which surrendered prisoners of war on the 19th October, 1781:—

To his Excellency Gen. George Washington:—

1 Lieut. General.	15 Adjutants.
1 Brigadier General.	20 Quarter-Masters.
2 Colonels.	14 Surgeons.
12 Lieut. Colonels.	22 Mates.
14 Majors.	445 Serjeants.
83 Captains.	5780 Rank and File.
132 Lieutenants.	187 Drummers and Fifers.
55 Ensigns.	9 Bombardiers.
4 Cornets.	6 Gunners.
2 Chaplains.	154 Matrosses.

Hospital Department.

1 Surgeon and Field Inspector.

3 Surgeons.	4 Stewards.
10 Mates.	2 Ward Masters.
2 Chaplains.	19 Assistants.
2 Purveyors.	2 Carpenters.

Commissary Department.

1 Commissary of Prisoners.	2 Clerks.
4 Commissary of Issues.	3 Issuers.
1 Commissary of Forage.	2 Coopers.
2 Assistants' Forage.	1 Labourer.

Total, 7025.

N. B. This return is exclusive of the warrant department, which adds upwards of 1000 to the list of prisoners.

One hundred square-rigged vessels, and upwards of 300 pieces of ordnance, 80 of which are brass.

During the siege the enemy's loss was* **00 killed, deserted, and made prisoners.

25th *Oct'r*, '81.—This morning, after breakfast, Lieut. Weitzel, Doyle,

* The edge of the manuscript has been accidentally burnt near the centre of the book.

and self, took a walk to town to spend the afternoon, but we could not procure any wine or spirits, for love or money. We then crossed the river in expectation of getting some there. We ranged through the whole town, but all to no purpose.

We also expected to see Mr. Jacob ***gler, who, I was informed, was on Gloucester side, and a Captain in Col. Connell's corps.

I have the above information from Lieut. Crarey, (a British Officer,) who was formerly a prisoner of war at Lancaster.

26th Oct'r, 81.—This day our brigade was ordered for fatigue, but the weather being rainy, and very stormy, and very cool, which prevented us as ordered.

27th.—This morning 10 o'clock our brigade mounted guard, and did several fatigues in town. Capt. Irwin, Lieut. Dixon, and self, had the Reserve Picquet. Spent the evening very agreeably, drinking wine, &c.

28th Oct'r, '81.—This day I was very unwell from last night's carouse.

This afternoon I received the following letters, viz:

One from Lieut. Francis White, dated York Town, Oct. 18, '81; one from Capt. J. Stake, dated do.

The above letters I received from Mr. Geiger.

29th.—This morning 9 o'clock our brigade went on fatigue to demolish the works we had the trouble to throw up when his lordship had possession of the town.

This evening the officers of our line received orders to make out lists of clothing that they wanted, in order that they might be supplied from the merchants in town.

30th Oct'r, '81.—This day Majors Edwards and Alexander, and Capt. Claypoole of our line, were chosen to purchase such clothing as would suit the officers of our line, from the merchants of York and Gloucester.

This day took a walk to town—our heavy pieces of ordnance putting on board.

This evening our agents sent to camp a fine parcel of white superfine broadcloth, linens, &c.

31st Oct'r, '81.—This day was very busily employed by our agents in completing our line with clothes, linens, &c.

A very cool day, and a little rain in the afternoon.

Nov'r 1st, '81.—This day our brigade went to town, mounted guard, and were employed in getting the military stores on board.

This afternoon a soldier (a wagoner) was killed, of the Infantry, by a shell bursting as he was rolling them out of the wagon, and four wounded, one mortally.

This evening bought half-a-dozen China cups and saucers, and one cream-pot, and one pound of excellent Green Tea, for which articles I paid four-milled dollars, for the use of our mess.

Spent the evening very agreeably with a number of gentlemen, drinking port wine, &c.

2nd Nov'r, '81.—This morning early our line and the Marylanders received orders to hold themselves in readiness to march on the 4th instant at sun-rise.

This day was very busily spent in dividing our clothing, &c.

3rd *Nov.*, '81.—This day a number of British and Hessian prisoners were marched out of town under the command of the New York troops.

This morning Lieut. Collier and self were to town, and bought the following articles for the use of our Mess, viz:

			Virginia Money.
To 3 lb. Bohea Tea at 12s. per lb.	.	.	£1 16s.
" 58 lb. Sugar, at 1s. 6d. per lb.	.	.	4 7
" 22 lb. Coffee, at 1s. 6d. per lb. .	.	.	1 13
" 2 bottles Mustard,	.	.	6
" 4 skeins Sewing Silk, .	.	.	4
" 1 silk Handkerchief,	.	.	18
			£9 4s.

4th *Nov'r.* Walked to town with Lieut. Tilden and Capt. Stevenson, to purchase some small articles. This day I drew the following articles of clothing, which we received from the merchants in York, at the following prices sterling, viz:

		Sterling.		
1 piece Linen, 25 yds., at 1s. 8½d. .	.	£2	2s.	8½d.
3¼ yds. Blue Cassimere, at 7s. 9d. .	.	1	5	2¼
** pairs Worsted Hose,	.	.	4	10
** pairs Cotton do., .	.	.	4	8
** pairs Silk do., .	.	.	10	0
12 yds. Cassimere, at 7s. 3d., .	.	1	5	5½
1 Black B. Handkerchief, .	.	.	3	6
1 yd. Russia Sheeting, .	.	.	1	5
Thread and Silk, .	.	.		10
2 yds. Mode at 1s. 10d.,	.	.	3	8
1 pair Shoes, .	.	.	4	6
1 pair Sleeve Buttons and Thread,	.	.	8	0¼
Trimmings, &c., .	.	.	12	6
Blackball and Soap, .	.	.	2	8½
			£7 10	00

This day sent the following letters to Pennsylvania, viz:

One to my Brother App., No. 11; one to Lieut. Johnston.

This morning received orders to march to-morrow morning, sun-rise.

5th *Nov'r*, '81—This day marched at eleven o'clock, A. M. Our line and the Maryland Regiments marched past Cheesecake Church and Burrell's Mills, and encamped within half a mile of said mills, being ten miles.

6th *Nov'r.*—This morning at sunrise the troops took up the line of march, passed Hickory Neck Church, when we got into one of our old routes, being 19 miles, and encamped at Bird's Ordinary. We also passed the Burnt Brewery.

7th *Nov'r.*—This morning at day-light the troops took up the line of march. I mounted the Provost Guard this morning, and had fifteen prisoners.

Encamped at Kent Court House, being 14 miles.

8th Nov'r.—The troops took up the line of March at sunrise this morning. Passed Savage's Farm, Frazer's Ordinary, and Bottom's Bridge, and encamped within half a mile of said bridge, being 10 miles.

9th.—This morning at day-light the troops took up the line of march, and encamped on the heights at Richmond, being 14 miles.

10th Nov'r.—This day the Maryland line crossed James' River. Took a walk to town this morning. Played billiards. Spent the afternoon at Mr. Galt's Ornery. Dined vevy sumptuously upon rock fish, &c.

11th Nov'r.—This day the artillery cross the river. A very rainy and disagreeable day.

12th Nov'r.—The Q'r. M'r. G'l. and stores crossed this day.

13th Nov'r.—This morning our Battalion crossed James' River at Richmond, landed at Manchester, and encamped within one mile of said town. In the afternoon E. Butler and self took a walk to town and played a few games at billiards.

14th.—This day Lieut. Collier and self crossed the river in order to purchase some small articles, &c.

Wrote a letter to my Brother App., No. 12. Spent the afternoon at the ornery, and playing billiards, continuing at the table all night.

15th Nov'r.—This day, 10 o'clock A. M., our line took up the line of march, and encamped near Osborn's Ware Houses, on James' River, being 15 miles.

I felt very unwell this whole day from last night's carouse.

16th.—This morning at day-break our line took up the line of march, passed Ware Church, and encamped near Appomattox River, being ten miles.

This afternoon Capt. Marshall, Lieut. Collier, and self, crossed the river in order to take a view of Petersburgh. Played billiards all the afternoon.

A number of our stores crossed this day.

17th Nov. '81.—This day our line crossed the Appomattox River and encamped half a mile from Petersburg. A very rainy and disagreeable day. Walked to town in the afternoon, and played a few games of billiards.

18th Nov. '81.—This day we remained on this ground, the men to wash their clothing and furbish up their arms, &c.

Lt. Collier and myself went to the river to catch a few of the scaly fry. This day I went on fatigue.

19th Nov.—This morning at sunrise the troops took up the line of march, and were joined by Lt. Col. White with about Two Hundred Horse—one half in front and the other half in the rear of the troop; passed through a very fine level country—passed Dinwiddie Court House, Stony creek, and encamped within half a miles of said bridge, being 19 miles.

20th Nov. '81.—The troops took up the line of march this morning;

a heavy frost; crossed Notaway River, Lew Jones's bridge, and encamped on said Jones's farm, Brunswick County, being 14 miles. No pines this day.

21st *Nov.* '81.—This morning at sunrise the troops took up the line of march and passed two small bridges—no pines.—Encamped on Earl Edmunds's farm—being 15 miles.

This morning I mounted the rear guard of the army, &c. Brunswick County.

Yesterday morning Ensign Beaty and Capt. Mentzer, of the Maryland line, fought a duel. The latter was shot through the head; died immediately.

22d *Nov.* The troops took up the line of march this morning at sunrise, crossed Mayherrin Creek, on a bad bridge made of rails,—no pines —and encamped near Mitchell's Ornery, Mecklenburg County, being 16 miles.

23d *Nov.*—This morning at sunrise, the troops took up the line of march, passed through a very good country, crossed Mill Creek, and encamped near Mitchell's Ornery, Mecklenburg County, being 12 miles.

24th *Nov.* '81.—This morning at sunrise the troops took up the line of march by the left, crossed Allen Creek, which was within half a mile of the ground we left this morning.

At about 11 o'clock, A. M., we arrived at Roanoke River—our Brigade being in front.—We immediately crossed by Regiments, and crossed all our baggage-wagons, &c., before sunset, being a march of eight miles, and encamped two miles on the south sides of the river. Total 10 miles.

N. B. The troops crossed at Taylor's Ferry, Mecklenburg County.

25th *Nov.* '81.—A very rainy and disagreeable day. This place abounds in deer and wild turkeys, &c.

26th *Nov.*—A very fine clear sunshiny day. This day dried and aired our clothes, &c., which got wet from yesterday's rain.

The men received orders to wash their clothes, &c., furbish up their arms for inspection this afternoon.

Lt. David Marshall of our battalion shot a very fine deer this afternoon, within one mile of our encampment.

27th *Nov.*—This morning at sunrise, Capt. Lewis and Lieut. Collier (my messmate) went a hunting for wild deer and turkeys—but brought home no game.

A very fine and clear day. Received orders to march to-morrow morning at sunrise.

28th *Nov.*—Last night and this morning it rained very hard, which prevented us from marching this day.

29th *Nov.* '81.—This morning at sunrise, the troops took up the line of march, passed through a fine level good country. Roads very sloppy. This day we marched * * * miles into North Carolina, and encamped near Williamsborough. The town is composed of one fine church, one tavern, one smith shop and five or six small log houses. Granville County. 10 miles.

Yesterday I wrote a letter to Lieut. Andrew Johnston.

30th Nov. '81.—This morning, Lieut. Reeves was left on the ground with a number of our sick.

The troops took up the line of march this morning at the usual time, and encamped at Harrisburg. The buildings are two elegant houses and a few ware-houses. Granville County. 12 miles.

December 1st, 1781.—This morning at sunrise the troops took up the line of march, it being excessive bad marching in consequence of last night's rain.

Passed through a very fine country; saw several very elegant orchards, peach and apple, and encamped on Gen. Carson's farms, which are the most elegant farms I have seen since we left Pennsylvania. He has also a very fine apple orchard in front of his mansion house. His buildings are but trifling. 13 miles. Granville County.

The above mentioned person has eighty-five thousand acres of land all in one tract.

2d Dec. '81.—The troops took up the line of march this morning at sunrise; passed through a very fine country; road very sloppy in consequence of last night's frost. We encamped near Pane's Ornery Caswell County. 16 miles.

3d Dec. '81.—This morning at sunrise, the troops took up the line of march; passed Caswell Court House, and crossed Hico Creek, a very tedious and disagreeable march; sloppy and hilly; encamped near said Court House and within a stone's throw of Mr. Black's Tavern, where I drank tolerably good beer. Caswell County. 10 miles.

This evening Lieuts. Dixon and Moore shot a very fine young deer, close by our encampment.

Likewise a soldier of our battalion shot a fine deer.

4th Dec'r.—The troops took up the line of march this morning at sunrise. The greater part of the road being very hilly, crossed Hico and Country Line Creek. A snow fell this day of about four inches deep. Encamped at Mr. Sumner's Ordinary.

Capt. Bartholomew, of our battalion, unfortunately broke his leg this evening. Caswell county. 18 miles.

5th Dec'r, '81.—This day we lay still in order to give our soldiers rest, as they were much fatigued from yesterday's march.

6th Dec'r.—This morning I had the honour of commanding the Bullock Guard. I marched with my detachment to one Mr. Davis's, about three miles from our encampment to get a fresh corn-field for the cattle, 402 in number.

7th Dec'r.—The troops took up the line of march this morning at sunrise, (I still being a Bullock Guard.) Passed through a very beautiful country, no pine to be seen. Very sloppy this morning. Crossed Haw River. The troops were obliged to ford it, which was very disagreeable this season of the year, and encamped on the banks of said river. 16 miles. Guilford county.

Our heavy baggage was left on the ground this morning, under the command of Major James Moore.

8th Dec'r, '81.—This morning at day-light the troops took up the line of march, passed through a very fair country (no pines,) and encamped at Guilford Court House. 20 miles.

N. B. Crossed a branch of Hico Creek, where we were obliged to make a bridge across on account of its being about four feet deep.

We encamped on the heights near Guilford Court House, where the late action was fought between Gen. Greene and Lord Cornwallis. We found on said fields a number of buts of muskets, &c.

Between the ordinary and the court house we see a negro's head sticking on a sapling on one side of the road, and his right hand side to a sapling on the opposite side. He was just hanged, then cut to pieces for killing a white man, &c.

9th Dec'r, '81.—This day we remained on the ground in expectation of getting clothing washed, but the weather turned out to be very rainy and disagreeable. This place is called the Irish settlement.

10th Decr, '81.—We received orders this morning to remain on the ground for to wash our clothing, &c. This day very rainy and disagreeably cold.

11th Dec'r.—This morning at sunrise the troops took up the line of march. Passed through a very fine country, (settled by Quakers, who have tolerable good plantations, &c.) Crossed two branches of Deep Creek, and encamped near Mr. Barney **iddle's, on the banks of **st's Creek. 15 miles. Guilford county.

12th Dec'r.—The troops took up the line of march this morning at the usual time; passed through a country settled by Germans, who have very good plantations, and a small quantity of meadow, which is seldom to be seen. (A few pines this day.) Left Moravian town, called Salem eight miles upon our right hand.

Yesterday Col Craig of the 3d Battalion, Penn'a, took the right of our Brigade, and this day our Battalion encamped upon the right as usual. (16 miles) long.

Encamped on the hill near Mr. McCreary's. Roane county.

13th Dec'r, '81.—This morning at sunrise the troops took up the line of march. Passed through a fine country, (no pines.) Crossed the Yadkin in boats. The soldiers and the baggage forded, and encamped within 1 mile of said river. 13 miles.

14th Dec'r.—The troops took up the line of march this morning at sunrise. Passed through Salisbury, which is a fine little town; two or three elegant houses; and encamped within half-a-mile of said town. 7 miles.

This evening Capt. Davis and Lieut. Collier went to town and spent the evening with Capt. Christr. Stake at Mr. Bream's, an old townsman of mine.

15th Dec'r.—The troops took up the line of march this morning at sunrise. Passed through a very fine country; went back to town this morning and wrote the following letters, viz:

One to my Brother App., No. 13, and one to my mother, and delivered them to Capt. Christ'r Stake. Encamped at Mr. Taylor's, Roane county. 12 miles.

16th Dec'r.—This morning at sunrise marched at the usual time; crossed Coddle Creek, and Mr. Pheiffer's Ornery, where Capt. Bower and self dined. Passed through a fine country, and encamped on Rocky Run. Mecklenburg county. 14 miles.

Within half a mile of our encampments was an Indian Town of the Catawbas Nation. They are but few in number at this place, about eighty. About four miles from this place, I am informed, their principal town is, where they have fifteen square miles of land. The land here is very good, and no pines.

17th Dec'r, '81.—This day remained on the ground in consequence of rain.

18th Dec'r.—This morning a very great frost. The troops took up the line of march at the usual hour, crossed Millet Creek, marched through Charlotte Town, and encamped within half a mile of said town. There are but three tolerable houses in town, and about one dozen of ordinary buildings, &c. Mecklenburg county. 13 miles.

This day I mounted camp guard.

19th Dec'r.—The troops took up the line of march this morning at sunrise, and crossed Mt. Copper Creek and several other small runs, and encamped this side of Glenn's Branch. We saw but very few houses this day. 15 miles. Mecklenburg county.

20th Dec'r.—This morning at sunrise the troops took up the line of march. Passed through a fine level country, and encamped at 12 mile creek, Indian Land, in South Carolina. 10 miles. Camden District.

Lieuts. Lodge, McKinney, Stricker, Van Court, and self took a ride about four miles from our encampment to see an Indian town of the Catawba Nation. We had a very long, tedious, and disagreeable ride, and all small Indian foot-paths and thick woods to ride through. We see one of their towns, but it was only the remains of a town, which was burnt by the British. We rode on half a mile farther, when we found a very fine bottom, but all the old houses evacuated.

We see three Indians in a canoe, coming down Catawba River. We hailed them, and brought them to, and asked them several questions.

They informed us the town was half-a-mile the other side of the river. We were very desirous of seeing the town, but could not trust our horses on this side for fear they would be stolen.

I marched the sick of our brigade this day.

We could not cross the creek, it being very high water in consequence of yesterday's rain. We were obliged to fall a number of trees across the creek for the troops to cross over.

21st Dec'r.—The troops took up the line of march at 12 o'clock, M. Crossed 12 mile creek, passed through a very fine country, and encamped at Maxwell Creek. 7 miles.

At this place were seventeen British officers, paroled. A warm day.

22nd Dec'r.—This morning at day-light the troops took up the line of march. Crossed Waxaw Creek, Cane Creek, Camp Creek, Gill's Creek, and Bear Creek, and encamped on the south side of said creek, on Major Barkley's farm, Creaven county, Camden District. 10 miles. This a very rainy, sloppy, and disagreeable day.

23rd Dec'r, '81.—This morning at sunrise the troops took up the line of march. Passed through a piney, and what they call Black Jack, a very fine, level road. See a number of wagons, &c., destroyed, and a number of buts of guns, &c., and encamped one mile on the south side of the Flat Rock. 20 miles. Camden District.

This is the ground where a number of our soldiers were cut to pieces by Mr. Tarlton's corps, on the retreat of Gen'l Gates.

March through a great part of the long-leafed pine. N. B. This place, called the Flat Rock, is about three acres in circumference, flat and solid.

24th Dec'r, '81.—The troops took up the line of march at the usual time. This day very disagreeable marching, rainy and very sloppy, and encamped within two miles of Camden, in the woods. 16 miles.

25th Dec'r, '81.—This day remained on the ground, the men being much fatigued, their clothes very dirty. Received an invitation to dine with Mr. Le Count. Seven other gentlemen besides myself. He has a very fine plantation. His house is built on an Indian monument, about ten feet high. We dined very sumptuously on a very elegant dinner, and plenty of good spirits.

Said Mr. Le Count lives about three miles off the south side of Camden.

I also took a view of the town, which is greatly destroyed by the enemy. There are yet three good houses remaining. The enemy had a number of outworks, which are all demolished.

This being one of the most remarkable Christmases that ever I experienced, very warm, &c., we passed the afternoon very agreeably, without fire in the parlour.

26th Dec'r, '81.—The troops took up the line of march this morning at sunrise. The Maryland troops and the heavy baggage were ordered to remain on the ground until we had crossed the river.

We passed through Camden, and crossed the Wateree, where we had but two scows to cross over troops and baggage, and encamped about two miles on the south side of said river in a piney woods, intermixed with a few Black Jacks. 5 miles.

27th Dec'r.—This morning at sunrise, the troops took up the line of march, passed through a very disagreeable swamp for about two miles, half leg deep in water. No house to be seen this day but one. Nothing but pines.

Encamped near one Mr. Reynolds, lately from Penn'a, a tenant of Col. Canshaw's. 10 miles.

This day I mounted the bullock guard.

Took up my quarters at one Mr. Bennet's, (a Quaker,) who treated me exceeding polite, and gave me every thing his house afforded. We lived very well, &c.

28th Dec'r.—This morning at sunrise our line marched (the Maryland being in the rear of us,) passed through a very fine level country, all long-leaf pine. This day we had a very fatiguing march, being very warm. See three or four tolerable good houses. Encamped within half a mile of Congaree River. 23 miles.

29th.—This morning at sunrise we crossed Congaree River, and encamped on the south of Col. Thompson's, (a gentleman who lives in great affluence.) Has a very elegant mansion house, which is surrounded by a number of negro houses.

The widow Mot and Mr. Dart live within sight of Col. Thompson's, on a very high hill. The situations of both places are very elegant. Orangeburg county. 5 miles.

This being a very fine, agreeable day, the woods all green. The cane swamps look exceeding beautiful. A long kind of a moss grows on the different kinds of the trees.

On the north side of the Congaree river a fine parcel of curious timber called Palmetto trees. It has long sharp leaves like the blades of Indian corn, from the bottom to the top, (no limbs) all leaves.

Dec. 30th, '81.—This morning at sunrise the troops took up the line of march; passed three or four houses near the road. A number of very fine ladies came to the road to take a view of us as we passed by. A very fine level road this day's march. All pines, intermingled with a few oaks and hickories.

Encamped in a German settlement (called Tories,) near one Mr. Adam Freitly's (a German,) who had a great number of negroes.

A very fine, warm, and agreeable day. Orange county—13 miles.

Dec. 31st.—The troops took up the line of march at sunrise—passed through a German settlement—passed a number of swamps—marched past Orangeburgh Town and encamped within a mile of said town. The enemy burnt the whole town except one house and the goal.

There are a number of militia, horse and foot, doing duty at this place, to keep the tories in order, commanded by Gen. Sumpter. Orangeburgh county—13 miles.

Yesterday evening we drew rice for forage for our horses.

Jan. 1st, 1782.—The troops took up a line of march this morning at sunrise. We were obliged to cross a number of very disagreeable swamps. No bridges could be made, and we were obliged to wade them knee deep. Very few houses on this day's march. Pines very high.

Just as we entered our encamping ground a flock of green parroquets flew through our encampment, which was a very great curiosity with us.

The trees here all green, just as they are in Pennsylvania in the spring, the willow, oak, pines, and a number of other trees, of which I cannot yet ascertain their names, but I can assure you the sight is very pleasing.

Encamped in the wilderness amongst a fine parcel of pines and surrounded by swamps, &c.—20 miles.

This day being very warm and agreeable so that I could have marched in my shirt sleeves.

Very low ground this whole day's march.

Very few oaks or hickories on this ground.

Jan. 2d, '82.—This morning at sunrise the troops took up the line of march; passed through a low, swampy and piney country. For about seven miles the country was exceeding level.

Only saw one or two houses, (they are not houses, but may be properly called huts,) and a great distance from the road side.

This evening after we had pitched our tent, a fine flock of green parroquets flew through camp.

After a long and fatiguing march we encamped in a —— piney woods, not a stick of other wood ; the smoke of which is as black as charcoal and very disagreeable.

Very likely for rain this evening. 15 miles.

N. B. Encamped within three miles of Edisto river.

Jan. 3d, '82.—This morning at nine o'clock the troops took up the line of march. This whole day's march was very disagreeable, through swamps and mud up to our knees.

Exceeding bad roads for wagons and artillery.

We crossed Edisto river, on which are erected two very elegant saw mills, four saws in each mill, and as they saw the boards, planks, &c., they throw them into the river, from which they take them to Charlestown. The river runs very rapid. There is also a grist mill erected on said river, joining with said saw mills.

No buildings on the farm adjoining said river but a few negro huts.

All the Virginia troops were discharged this day, so that the Virginians have not a single soldier left in the field.

Encamped on Hickory Ridge within four miles of Gen. Greene's army—10 miles.

This evening the frogs in the swamp sang very sweetly.

Jan. 4th, 1782.—A very heavy dew and fog this morning.

The troops took up the line of march at the usual hour. This whole day's march swamps as usual.

Joined Gen. Greene's army this morning at eleven o'clock.

Encamped in the woods at Round O—5 miles.

Jan. 5th, 1782.—Yesterday Gens. Greene, Wayne, Gist and a number of other gentlemen officers went about fifteen miles into the country from camp to an elegant entertainment.

This morning and all last night a very heavy dew which is very unwholesome. This day very warm.

Jan. 6th, '82.—The water here is very bad, no springs or rivulets, all ponds and swamps, which are full of little insects ; in consequence of which I attempted to dig a well about ten yards from our tent. I dug about four feet deep, when I found I was very successful in getting tolerable good water, cool and clear.

This day I wrote the following letters, viz : one to my brother App. No. 14 ; one to Lieut. Johnston of our Regiment ; sent them by Capt. Kirkwood of the Delaware State.

Dr. Davis, Mr. Furgeson and Mr. Baker, the latter are gentlemen inhabitants of this state, and the Doctor a brother of Capt. Davis's—the above gentlemen spent the afternoon and drank tea with us. We received very warm invitations to come and see them, which opportunity I mean to embrace in a few days. This day excessive warm.

This country here abounds in wild deer, geese, ducks, &c. The geese and ducks roost in the rice fields, which are at present (or in winter, as they call this season) all overflowed with water.

Jan. 7th '82.—This day very warm. The country here abounds in turkey-buzzards, crows, ravens, and the blackbirds are innumerable.

There is Five Pounds fine for shooting a turkey-buzzard.

Jan. 8th, '82.—This day received an invitation to dine with Capt.

Andrew, an inhabitant, about two miles from camp. To morrow is appointed for that purpose. This day very warm.

Went to see Capt. Hall and Dr. Blithe of the North Carolina line.

This evening at sunset we received orders to march to morrow morning at eight o'clock, which was disagreeable news to me and others.

Jan. 9th, '82.—This morning at eight o'clock our Brigade took up the line of march. The roads exceeding good, it was impossible for roads to be better, and very straight and level, just like a bowling green. See a number of elegant houses, all a short distance from the road, also a number of plantations which are all overflowed with water, and ditches dug round them to drain off the water.

Marched through Jacksonborough in which are built four or five tolerable good frame houses and a number of smaller houses; and encamped within a quarter of a mile of said town—13 miles.

I had the pleasure of being the advance guard of our Brigade, and after we arrived at our ground was obliged to mount Governor Rutledge's guard in town, where I had the pleasure of spending the afterternoon and part of the night with the Governor and a number of the members of Assembly, and half a dozen of very agreeable ladies; had plenty of good Maderia wine and spirits, which a few day ago came from Charleston.

Our Brigade was sent to this place to protect the Assembly whilst sitting.

Jan. 10th, '82.—This day our Brigade moved about two hundred yards in the rear of our former encampment, in consequence of our first situation's being rather disagreeable, the ground being rather wet and sloppy.

Jan. 11th, '82. This day we made ourselves a very fine bedstead—dug a well about seven feet deep about three yards from our boys' tent, and now promising ourselves to live like Christians again.

This day we were under the disagreeable necessity of drawing all rice instead of Indian Meal, and it is a very poor substitute for bread, and it is a mystery to see how to make it into bread.

The Carolinians say they are fonder of rice bread than they are of the best wheat.

Jan. 12th.—This morning we received orders to hold ourselves in readiness to march at the shortest notice; in the evening we struck our tents, loaded our baggage, crossed Pon-Pon, marched all night, and in the morning one hour before daylight we arrived within half a mile of Stoneo Ferry, Col. Lawrence's Infantry in front of us, who were to surprise a party of four hundred foot and sixty horse, who were fortifying themselves on John's Island. Our plan fell through, daylight appearing and a number of Infantry not having crossed the marsh. Said marsh being very disagreeable crossing, it was middle deep with mud, weeds and water, a number of our Infantry stuck fast and were obliged to be pulled out, &c. Our Brigade was to support the Infantry—22 miles.

Jan. 13th, '82.—This morning about daylight the Infantry and our line marched about one mile and a half from Stoneo Ferry—lay upon our arms all day. Weather cold and disagreeable. No tents or baggage

This day the remaining part of the army joined us.

Jan. 14*th*, '82.—This day we built a very fine brush hut. About 11 o'clock, A. M., two of our six pounders were ordered to the Public Landing, (about one mile from Stoneo Ferry) in order to drive away a row-galley which lay at anchor in Stoneo River, to prevent our troops from crossing on John's Island at low water. Our artillery threw up a small breast work along side of the marsh, the distance was about half a mile, our field pieces fired about a dozen of shot at the galley, three of which struck her, to which I, Major Kean, Lieut. McPherson and a number of other gentlemen had the pleasure of being eye-witnesses. After receiving a shot or two she fired several shot (an eighteen pounder) and dropped slowly down the river.

This evening Maj. Edwards, Lieut. Marchand and about twenty four privates went on John's Island and found the enemy had evacuated it and left a number of stores behind them; wine was one of the articles.

Lieut. McPherson and self walked to Stoneo Ferry, where we found one mansion-house and a number of stores evacuated. We searched them and found them all plundered, the furniture broke to pieces—in one of the storehouses was left about two hundred weight of good cotton.

This day we drew Indian meal again. Excessive cold weather this day.

Jan'y. 15*th*, '82.—This day's orders, no officer or soldier to leave camp on any account. We were informed the enemy were out in force this day, in consequence of which we marched about four miles towards Charlestown, and returned to our former encampment. 8 miles.

Jan'y. 16*th*.—This morning at sunrise the whole army took up the line of march, for Jacksonsburgh it was thought, but to our great mortification we found we were disappointed, and encamped in the woods near Mr. Frazor's farm and about four miles from Jacksonsburgh; lay in the woods without our tents. This day we were obliged to wade a number of very disagreeable puddles. Very cool this day. 15 miles.

Jan'y. 17*th*, '82.—This day our mess built a brush hut for ourselves to shelter us from the weather. (To be sure, and a poor substitute it is.) This afternoon the officers of our Brigade dined with Capt. Lusk's mess; we spent the afternoon and part of the evening very agreeably, drinking grog, &c.

Our encampment is surrounded by rice plantations, which are all overflowed with water, and in which ponds, as we may call them, there are the greatest plenty of wild ducks that ever I see, thousands in one flock.

Jan'y. 18*th*, '82.—This morning I had the pleasure of mounting the Provost Guard, in front of Mr. Frazor's dwelling house. (It is a two story brick house.) This afternoon I received five prisoners of war, who were taken on James's Island.

A very rainy and disagreeable day.

There are a number of very elegant buildings close to our encampment—the inhabitants very polite and genteel. Balls almost every evening.

Jan'y. 19*th*.—This morning about two o'clock I had a small fire kindled to myself near my guard. I was very agreeably entertained by the singing of a very fine bird called the large Gray Owl. He sang very melodious for about two hours. Very heavy firing yesterday morning, cannon and small arms. The firing was at Genl. Greene and his party of Horse who were within one mile of Charlestown, reconnoitring, &c.

Jan'y. 20th, '82.—This morning Lt. Doyle and self went to the borough where our heavy baggage was left to get some clean clothes, &c; dined very sumptuously with Col. Craig. Roads very sloppy.

This day Governor Burke of North Carolina arrived at Head Quarters, who a few days ago made his escape from James's Island. He was paroled on said Island.

This afternoon all the field officers of the army were called upon in council to inquire into the conduct of Governor Burke, whether he was justifiable in making his escape from the enemy whilst on parole.

Jan'y. 21st, '82.—This morning very cool. It was reported this day that the Board of Officers which sat yesterday, gave it in favour of Govr. Burke that he was justifiable in making his escape from the enemy.

Jan'y. 22d.—This morning we had a white frost.

After breakfast Lts. Doyle, McDowell, Allison and self took a walk to the country (about four miles) where we found a number of Carolina soldiers straggling through the country, which is against General Orders. We were taking a view of one of their rice mills, where they shell their rice. We heard a musket fired, we pursued three of said soldiers and caught two of them, who had shot one of the poor negroes' hogs. We guarded them to camp and had them confined.

Jan'y. 23d, '82—This morning Lt. Doyle, Ball and self walked to our baggage, which was at Jacksonsburgh, to get some clean clothes. 5 miles.

This evening our baggage arrived from camp.

We are ordered in this day's General Orders to deliver all our tents and camp-kettles to the Qr. Mr. Gl.

This day received the following letters, viz: One from my brother Frederick dated the 6th Decr. '81; one from my sister Nancy dated 6th Decr., '81.

Jan'y. 24th, '82.—This morning 10 o'clock the whole army, (except the Light Infantry which lay about ten miles from the main army,) took up the line of march and encamped within a mile of our old encampment, opposite Mr. Frazor's seat. Nothing but pines here to burn for firewood, which is very disagreeable.

This afternoon the Third or Col. Craig's Battalion of our line was ordered to Jacksonsburgh for the protection of the Assembly of this State, who are now sitting in said borough.

They were alarmed last night, which was the reason of a reinforcement's being sent them.

Jan'y. 25th, '82.—This morning I had the pleasure of mounting the Rear Guard of the Army; disposed of my sentinels as I though proper, no officer of the day appearing on the Grand Parade. My guard consisted of 2 S, 2 C, 2 D and F, and 24 Privates.

This day whilst on guard I received a letter from Mr. Bandow, dated at Lancaster the 6th Dec'r. '81. Last night a very heavy frost.

There is a very beautiful bird in this country called a Red Bird. It is all red and has a black cap on its head. It is the bigness of a mocking bird.

Jan'y 26th.—This morning I was relieved by Lieut. Dixon. A very cool day; ice about half an inch thick.

Jan'y 27th, '82. Nothing material this day. Very windy and cold. The weather very changeable.

Jan'y 28th.—This day a Subaltern and a Surgeon from the British army came to Head Quarters. For what reason they left Charleston I cannot yet ascertain.

It is thought the enemy will soon evacuate the city.

Jan'y 29th.—This day Lieuts. Collier, Hammond, and self, received an invitation to dine at Head Quarters. We accepted the invitation, dined very sumptuously. Spent the afternoon very agreeably, drinking wine, &c.

Jan'y 30th.—Last night was as cold as ever I experienced to the northward. This morning I rode to a shelling-mill, (Rice,) in order to procure some boards to make a bed for our mess, to keep us from lying on the cold ground. A very cold day. Floored our tent, and built a very fine chimney to our tent.

Jan'y 31st, '82.—This whole day I employed in writing letters to my friends, &c., viz: One to my brother Michael App, No. 15; one to my mother; one to my sister Nancy Kneass; one to my friend Capt. John Doyle; and sent them by Lieut. Pendergast, who promised to deliver them.

Feb'y 1st, '82.—A very rainy and very disagreeable day.

Feb'y 2nd, '82.—This morning I had the pleasure of mounting the rear picquet of the army. Five deserters passed my guard (all Scotchmen,) on their way to Virginia. This day very cloudy.

Feb'y 3rd, '82.—This morning I was relieved by a Maryland officer. Very likely for rain this day. If the weather in this country clears up, and the sun shines before 12 o'clock, M., it is a sure sign of rain that day; but if the weather clears, and the sun shines after 12 o'clock, it is a very true symptom of a clear day.

Feb'y 4th, '82.—This evening Major James Moore arrived with our heavy baggage and two pieces of artillery, &c. They brought with them two British officers, who were taken going through the country as a flag to settle some of their private affairs.

A few days ago a spy was taken looking through our army, and is now under guard at Jacksonsburgh.

Feb'y 15th, 82.—This day I wrote the following letters, viz: One to my brother Frederick; one to my cousin Harry Dering; and one to Mr. W. B.

Sent the above letters by Col. Otho Williams, inclosed in a letter to Mr. Nichs. Hower, Frederick Town, Maryland.

Feb'y 6th, '82.—A few days ago I had the pleasure of seeing a young alligator, about one foot long. They are the same shape as a man-eater or a lizard, only the alligators have a sort of gills.

This afternoon Capt. Smith Stodsbury and Lieut. White, joined the southern army, with a number of men who were left sick at Williamsburgh, Virg'a. Rainy and cloudy.

Feb'y 7th, '82.—This day twelve deserters came to Head Quarters.

The enemy came out as far as Beacon's Bridge, two miles this side of Dorchester, which is twenty miles from Charleston, and twenty-three miles from this place. All day very cloudy and rainy.

This afternoon Lieut. Dennis's waiter killed a very large rattle-snake. It was above six feet long, and of a prodigious thickness.

Feb'y 8th, '82.—A very rainy and disagreeable, dull day.

Feb'y 9th, '82.—This day another rattle-snake, of about five feet two inches, was killed in the rear of our encampment, by the same person. A fine and clear day.

Feb'y 10th, '82.—A very rainy and disagreeable day, so that every person was obliged to stay in their tents. This day I got a suit of regimentals finished.

Feb'y 11th.—A very fine, clear, and warm day.

Feb'y 12th.—This morning at day-light the army was under arms in consequence of the enemy's movements.

This day I mounted the Rear Guard of the army.

Feb'y 13th.—A very fine, warm, and pleasant day.

Feb'y 14th, '82—No particular occurrences this day.

Feb'y 15th, '82.—This day a number of our Infantry came from the lines.

The peach and plumb blossoms in full bloom.

Feb'y 16th.—Five Hessian deserters came this day from the Savannah.

This day I was very much fatigued playing cricket.

Feb'y 17th.—A very fine, agreeable, warm day. There is a tree in this country called the Pride of America. It is full of berries, which hang in clusters. These trees are always full of birds of different kinds, and [who] eat those berries.

Feb'y 18th.—A fine and warm day. This day Mr. Frazer presented me with a curious smoke pipe, which is made of a brier root, called Bam-boo.

Feb'y 19th.—This morning we had a heavy rain. The afternoon cleared up very fine.

This evening I went on command to Col. Haines's farm, whose lot it was to fall unfortunately into our cruel enemy's hands, and was hung by those damnable murderers. Said Haines left a family of very fine, promising children behind him, both motherless and fatherless. Gov. Hutchinson has the care of the estate.

I was ordered to take charge of the military stores, with a sergeant, corporal, and eighteen privates.

The situation of this farm is very agreeable. A very elegant mansion house and an overseer's house surrounded by negro houses, a very fine brick rice mill, store house, &c. A fine pond of water all around the house, which affords a great quantity of fish and wild ducks. From the main road to said house is a very beautiful avenue of about a mile long.

The plantation is about three miles from Jacksonsburgh. A garden full of very fine flowers, &c.

Feb'y 20th, '82.—Rained very hard all last night, and part of this morning. Cleared up in the afternoon very warm. Spent the evening very agreeably with Gen. Barnwell, Gov. Hutson, and five or six Assembly and Senate gentry. We sat up until eleven o'clock at night, drinking excellent Jamaica Grog and super-excellent French Brandy in its purity.

Feb'y 21st.—This morning very foggy. A very fine and warm day. This evening the officer came whom I was to relieve.

Feb'y 22nd, '82.—This evening we had a very agreeable dance at Major Moore's Bowery

A number of ladies came in from the country. Amongst the number were the Miss Couliets, Miss Glover, Miss Williams, the Miss Ellits, and a number of others whose names I cannot recollect. Amongst the number was a Miss Miles, who could neither speak nor hear, and could perform her dancing to admiration.

23d Feb'y, '82.—This day I rode to Col. Craig's Regiment. Spent the afternoon very agreeably, playing cricket, &c.

24th Feb'y, '82.—This day Lieuts. Collier, White, and Stricker, came to see me at my quarters. They dined with me, &c. Spent the evening very agreeably with a number of Assembly men, drinking good grog, &c.

25th Feb'y, '82.—This day I rode to camp and reported my situation to the D. A. G., my men not having either arms or clothing. My guard consisted of North Carolina soldiers, &c.

The garden here is full of beautiful flowers of different kinds.

26th Feb'y.—This day I was relieved by Lieut. Wilkins of the Artillery, who had orders to make ten thousand blank cartridges with all possible despatch.

Received very warm invitations from Gov. Hutson to come and visit him.

27th Feb'y.—This day I went on General Court Martial of the S. Army.

28th Feb'y.—The army who are off duty are daily manœuvring in front of the D. A. G'l.

March 1st, '82.—This day five soldiers were executed, four for desertion, and one for marauding.

March 2nd.—A very heavy rain last night. A very dull, rainy, and cool day.

March 3d.—A very dull day, and likely for rain.

March 4th, '82. This morning at eleven o'clock the army was reviewed by Gen'l Greene; several manœuvres performed. The whole fired four rounds, one round by platoons, one round by divisions, and two rounds by battalions.

Rained a little in the afternoon.

The troops performed their several manœuvres with the greatest exactness and regularity.

March 5th, '82. In this day's orders Gen. Greene returns his thanks to the troops for their improvement in the several manœuvres performed yesterday; and the troops to hold themselves in readiness to march to-morrow, eight o'clock, if the weather will permit.

Two soldiers in the Maryland line were pardoned in this day's orders, who were to suffer death for that villainous crime of marauding.

A rainy and very dull day.

A few days ago Gen. Marion, it is said, was surprised by the enemy; very little execution done. Last evening two deserters came to Head Quarters.

March 6th, '82.—Last night very heavy rain and thunder and lightning.

All this day rain.—Our march is postponed until further orders.

March 7th.—This day rain and very disagreeable. One hundred and seventy North Carolinians joined us this day without arms.

This afternoon went to see Mr. Frazer's garden, which is very elegant, full of different kind of flowers, &c., a few lemon trees, fig trees, and a great variety of others. At the foot of the garden is an elegant fish pond, which produces a number of fine trout, perch, &c.

March 8th.—Rained all day.

March 9th.—A very fine, clear, and warm day. Played a few games of fives.

March 10th. A rainy and dull day. Two Scotch deserters came to to the A. D. Genl's. this day.

March 11th.—Rained last night and a little this morning. Cleared up a fine day.

See a number of swallows or martins.

March 12th.—This day a second arrangement took place in our line. We were reduced to two battalions of eight companies each. A number of our officers left supernumerary, who are to retire to Penn'a. Rained and a very dull day.

March 13th.—This day Col. Craig, Capts. Wilkin and Claypoole, Major Alexander, Lieuts. Ball, Thornbury, Peeble, Dixon, Stricker, Gillchrist and Dr. Magee set off for Penn'a.

This day I wrote the following letters, viz: One to my mother; one to my brother App. No. 16; one to my cousin Henry Dering; one to Capt. J. Stake, and one to Capt. J. Doyle, and sent them by Lieut. Dixon.

This day it was currently reported that the enemy had evacuated the Quarter House, burnt all their works, returned to the city, and that two regiments had embarked. Cloudy all day.

14th March, '82.—This morning very fine and warm, agreeable; rained excessive hard in the afternoon; we were almost overflowed in our tents.

15th March.—This morning very clear—the afternoon very cloudy and like for rain.

This day we sent a wagon for oysters.

This evening Major Moore with a large detachment from the army went to the lines.

March 16th, '82.—This morning received an invitation from Lieut.

Smith to spend St. Patrick's day with him to-morrow in company with Lt. North, Lt. McCollam, Lt. Reed, Dr. McDowell, Ensigns Van Court and Cunningham. We rode to a Mr. Kennedy's, about fifteen miles from camp, at a place called Rantholes on Stoneo River, about twelve miles from Charleston, which place was very dangerous for us to remain longer than evening and we being at a tory's house. Spent the day and greater part of the night very agreeably.

17*th March*, '82.—Went to see a Mr. Williamson's garden, about a mile from Mr. Kennedy's, which is very beautifully laid out in beds and walks, surrounded by box; in the centre of which he has a very large fish-pond, which produces a variety of the scaly fry and wild ducks. After having satisfied our curiosity with the garden, plucked a few of the finest flowers and sweet scented shrubs, &c., we returned to Mr. Kennedy's—when dinner was laid—dined very sumptuously upon cod-fish, Irish potatoes, asparagus, fowls, &c.

After dinner we surrounded a large table, which was decked with good Nantes Brandy, excellent spirits, &c. We then went to work in form, chose a President and proceeded to business. Spent the afternoon and greater part of the night very agreeably.

March 18*th*, '82.—This morning after breakfast we started from Mr. Kennedy's, a little elevated with egg-nog, and unanimously agreed to call upon Mr. Williamson to compliment him on the elegance of his garden. We only intended to call and take a drink of grog with him, but he insisted upon our staying to dine with him and spend the after-noon, which we agreed to. After dinner we smoked our pipes, sang a song and got damnably drunk. On our starting, a short distance from the house my horse threw me and ran away. The rest of the company pursued him, but could not overtake him until he arrived at Mr. Ken-nedy's, which was about a mile. There we were all obliged to remain until we recovered, and came a little to our senses, which was about two o'clock in the morning.

March 19*th*, '82.—This morning about day-light we arrived in camp, when we adjourned to Mr. President's tent (Dr. McDowell;) we brought half a dozen of bottles of spirits with us; there we drank again until we were merry; slept greater part of the day.

March 20*th*, '82.—This whole day I was very unwell, being much bruised, falling from my horse.

March 21*st*.—A very heavy storm and rain last night. Mounted the camp guard this day. This day's orders; the army to hold themselves in readiness to march to-morrow morning 9 o'clock.

March 22*d*.—This morning the troops took up the line of march agreeable to yesterday's orders. Very sloppy roads all day. In this day's march we passed a hill, which was the first one I saw since we came to this state; passed Stoneo Church and encamped within a mile on the east side of said church on the road to Bacon's Bridge. 10 miles. This day Capt. Steel joined us.

23*d March*, '82.—This day was very busily employed by ourselves and men in building huts and chimneys. We built a very elegant brick chimney to our tent.

March 24th, '82.—This morning at nine o'clock the army took up the line of march agreeable to yesterday's orders—marched through a beautiful level country, roads very straight and good, and encamped in a wilderness in a thicket of brush, &c., about one mile from Bacon's Bridge. 10 miles.

March 25th.—This afternoon Lt. Collier and self went to pay a visit to the Infantry, who then lay at Bacon's Bridge (a very advantageous post.) On our arrival there we found they (Infantry) had just marched for Dorchester. After taking a view of the bridge, &c. we were obliged to return to our encampment again through a very heavy and disagreeable rain ; got wet thoroughly ; rained all the afternoon.

March 26th, '82.—This day was very busily employed by both officers and soldiers in building huts, raising tents, clearing the encampment, &c.

This afternoon we drew spirits. This evening a detachment went out under the command of Capt. Willmot, of the Maryland line. Our officers were very much dissatisfied with such partiality.

March 27th, '82.—This morning I mounted camp guard upon the left flank of our line. A fine and warm day.

March 28th, '82.—This day Lieuts. Smith, Reed, Van Court, and self, took a ride to Mr. Williamson's, about fourteen miles from camp, In the evening a very heavy rain, so that we were obliged to remain all night at Mr. Williamson's, who insisted on our staying, which we consented to. Spent the evening very agreeably, chatting and smoking a pipe, and drinking a glass of good grog.

This day the following memorial was sent to Gen. Greene in consequence of Capt. Willmot and Subalterns' going on command, viz :

CAMP, 28th March, 1782.

SIR :—When the subjects of a State conceive their rights infringed on, they readily suppose it arises from some mistake in the Executive part of the Government, or that the Governor means to adopt a mode of governing altogether new, and what the subjects have hitherto been unacquainted with. It is natural for the good subjects (as men who have a sense of subordination, knowing it to be the basis on which the privileges and happiness of the people so much depend, and more particularly in an army,) to inquire and modestly ask an explanation.

In the situation of injured subjects, do the Captains and Subalterns of the Pennsylvania line view themselves, when they reflect on the circumstances attending the formation of Capt. Willmot's detachment. We do therefore beg the General will inform us whether it was his intention that Capt. Willmot's command should be formed on the principle it was, or whether by mistake. Should it prove the latter, we shall be happy, and have not a doubt that Gen'l Greene's sense of equity and honor will lead him to do justice to the feelings of a body of injured Officers.

For the purpose of better explaining the points wherein we conceive ourselves agrieved, we enclose a copy of the order.

[Here is a blank page in the MS.]
5*

We have the honor to be with respect your obedient and very humble servants. (Signed,)

John Davis, Captain.	J. Steel, Capt.
Jos. Collier, Lieut.	W. Feltman, Lieut.
Henry Henly, Lieut.	Francis White, Lieut.
A. M. Dunn, Lieut.	Jas. McCulloch, Lieut.
Jno. Humphrey, Ensign.	Peter Cunningham, Lieut.
Samuel Smith, Capt.	Jacob Weitzel, Lieut.
H'y Bicker, Capt.	George North, Lieut.
J. McCullam, Lieut.	Jno. McKinney, Lieut.
T. Boude, Capt.	Thos. Doyle, Lieut.
J. Stotsbury, Capt.	Jno. Markland, Lieut.
Eben'r Denny, Ensign.	D McKnight, Lieut.
T. B. Tilden, Lieut.	James McPherson, Lieut.
Andrew Irwin, Capt.	J. Bowen, Capt.
T. Campbell, Capt.	R. Allison, Lieut.
B. Lodge, Lieut.	Wm. Lusk, Capt.
Jerr'h Jackson, Capt.	W. Bevins, Lieut.
Jno. Van Court, Ensign.	D. Marshall, Lieut.
James McFarlane, Lieut.	P. Smith, Lieut.

March 29th, 1782.—This morning it was excessive cold, snowed a little; cleared up a fine day. This morning we breakfasted at Mr. Williamson's; started about eleven o'clock, A. M., and arrived in camp about dinner time. Mr. Williamson was so good as to make us a present of an elegant bunch of asparagus.

This afternoon received an answer from Gen. Greene, in consequence of yesterday's memorial, viz:

HEAD QUARTERS, March 29th, 1782.

GENTLEMEN :—The constitution of an army and that of civil government are upon such different principles, the object of one so different from the other, that what might be essential to military operations in the formation of an army, would be found too simple for the various interests and different claims under civil government. The business of an army is to cover the country and annoy the enemy; that of civil government to protect and secure the rights of individuals. Therefore to argue from analogy of the rights of men under these different governments, is confounding things that have no relation, and reasoning upon principles that never can be admitted in an army. It is necessary both to the success and the security of an army, that its movements should be simple and secret. If the constitution of an army is not upon this principle, it can never answer the designs of government; and to form an army upon any plan which must defeat the great object of it, will burthen the community with great expense without utility. I am always as tender of the feelings of officers as possible; but if they go into refinements, and urge injuries which have no foundation but from improper modes of reasoning, I cannot sacrifice the public good and the reputation of the army at large to accommodate military operations to their way of thinking

You are to consider yourselves as officers of the continental army, bound by its laws, and governed by military maxims. You are under military, not civil, government. If you feel any injury, it must be as officers of the line of the army, and not those of any particular state. But if you will give yourselves the trouble to read military authors, and consider the practice of other armies, and reflect without prejudice upon the nature and design of detachments, you cannot but be convinced your grievances are imaginary

When detachments are made, it is for some particular purpose. To make it, therefore, in a manner not perfectly calculated to answer the design, would both sacrifice the public good, and by degrees the reputation of the army. There are more things to be taken into consideration in making a detachment than merely the military abilities of the officer commanding, or his rank in the line of the army.

There is a knowledge of the country, the people, and other local circumstances, which are very material considerations, to be attended to, to give success to an enterprise.

A man of an inferior capacity, with a knowledge of these things, would be able to execute and command much better with them, than a man of superior capacity without them.

I have ever made it a rule, and I find it well warranted by the best military writers, as well as from the reason and nature of the thing, to detach such men and officers as I may think requisite for the service to be performed. Nothing short of this can give success to an enterprise. I hope, therefore you will consider this explanation satisfactory. You may be assured I have the strongest disposition to oblige and do justice to the merit and services of every officer, but I must confine myself to such maxims of military government as are necessary to do justice to the public and the army at large.

I am, Gentlemen,

Your most obed't, humble serv't,

NATH. GREENE.

⌐o CAPT. JOHN DAVIS and others, of the Penn'a Line.

March 29*th continued*, 1782.—This afternoon Capt. Zigler joined our Regiment.

March 30*th*, '82.—A very cold and disagreeable day.

March 31*st*, 1782.—Morning and evening very cold.

Capt. Zigler ordered in this day's order to take command of Capt. Stevenson's company.

April 1*st*, 1782.—This day I wrote the following letters, viz : one to my mother; one to Capt. John Doyle; and one to Capt. Abraham Dehuff.

This morning I mounted the right flank picquet, about one mile from our encampment.

This evening received a letter from my brother App. This afternoon a Hessian Yeager (a deserter) passed my picquet. Our line mustered.

April 2*nd*, '82.—This morning a very heavy white frost

This day wrote the following letters, viz : one to my brother App.

No. 17 ; and one to my brother Kneass, No. 1 ; and sent them with the rest of the letters I wrote yesterday by Joseph ———, from Heiger's Town, Penn'a.

This evening received orders to gear up our wagon horses, and hold ourselves in readiness to march at a moment's warning. It is thought the enemy are determined to fight us, as they are making all preparations for that purpose.

This morning and evening very cool, and the middle of the day very warm.

Last night six soldiers, prisoners of war, made their escape out of the Provost Guard.

April 3rd, 1782.—Last night it was very cold.

This morning we sent an answer to Gen. Greene's letter of the 29th of last month, viz :

Camp, Apl. 3d, '82.

Sir :—That civil and military governments differ we grant. But that they are both constituted on principles of justice is a circumstance in itself too evident to admit of a doubt.

Therefore to quote civil government, and deduce thence that a subject, though not of a *State*, we had right to ask redress of grievances, and not to be deemed unreasonable. For that military subjects have not a claim to justice, although the Government is supposed to hold it in its very principles, is a matter that we have never yet been acquainted with. From what circumstances the General judges, when he supposes us to have taken up the matter as Officers of a State, and not of the Continental Army, we are at a loss to know ; and can only answer, that it is not in our power to account for the feelings and ideas of any body but ourselves ; but offer to explain why it should affect us particularly, as there was an officer of our brigade sent by regular detail with the detachment to the Grand Parade, and was dismissed thence by Capt. Willmot, who produced an order vesting him (Capt. Willmot) with power to approve of or reject such officers as he might think proper.

If the Gen'l will reflect a moment on the circumstances, he must naturally conclude, (unless he supposes us void of every delicate sensation) that we have cause of complaint. We conclude with answering, that although the answer to our address was not so satisfactory as we could have expected, we are induced, from the peculiar situation of the army, and our zeal for the public good, to decline any further steps on the occasion. And remain with respect,

Your most obedient humble serv'ts,

[Signed on behalf of the officers,]

John Davis, Capt. 1st Penn'a. Batt.
J. Bower, Capt. 2nd Penn'a. Batt.

This day a flag came to Bacon's Bridge.

April 4th, '82.—Lt. Collier, Doyle, and self, took a walk about a mile on the left of our encampment, crossed Ashley River, went to a Mr.

Itzer's house, drank grog, &c. A warm day. This day a second flag came to the bridge.

This day wrote the following letters, viz: one to my mother, and one to my brother App., No. 18, and sent them by Mr. Patton.

April 5th.—This day the Light Infantry broke up and joined their respective regiments.

This afternoon a third flag came to the bridge, requesting that the confiscated estates should not be sold, but restored to the proper owners, &c.

A very warm and fine day.

April 6th.—A very fine, warm, and agreeable day.

April 7th, '82.—This morning mounted Gen. Greene's guard. Lived exceedingly well; plenty of good wine, &c.

This day two deserters came to Head Quarters. A very warm day.

April 8th, '82.—Last night very cold. This morning a British Dragoon came to Head Quarters, who deserted last night from a party of two hundred horse, who came as far as Dorchester. He brought his horse and all his accoutrements with him.

This morning was relieved by Lieut. Hammond, of our regiment. This morning a very heavy firing of cannon and small arms.

April 9th, '82.—A very rainy and very disagreeable day. We were obliged to keep in our tents. In this day's General Orders I was appointed Paymaster to the First Battalion of Pennsy'a.

April 10th, '82.—All last night excessive hard rain, thunder and lightning. A cloudy, rainy, and dull day.

April 11th.—Rained all day. Last night a very heavy rain.

This afternoon a flag came to Bacon's Bridge.

April 12th, '82.—This morning Capt. Zigler went as a flag to the enemy's lines. Cloudy all day.

April 13th, '82.—This morning nine o'clock the whole army formed in a field in front of the Adjt. Genl's. Fired one round by platoons, one by divisions, and one by battalions.

A very fine, warm, and agreeable day.

April 14th, '82.—Last night it rained very hard, and very heavy thunder and lightning.

A fine, warm, and agreeable day.

April 15th.—This being a very warm day in camp, Lieuts. Doyle, Collier, and self, took a walk through the woods, and called at one Mr. Warren's house, where part of the fields were surrounded by palmetto trees, as a substitute for a fence. It has leaves about two feet long, and two inches wide, and very sharp at the end. The woods are all covered over with a very fine, sweet flower, called jessamine.

16th April.—A fine and warm day. Morning and evening very cool.

April 17th.—This evening a Capt. Orendorff and fifty men went to the lines.

April 18th, '82.—Spent the afternoon very agreeably with Lt. Clemens, of the Maryland line. This day four deserters came to Head Quarters.

April 19th, '82.—This day Lieut. McFarland and self took a ride into the country. Had the pleasure of seeing three alligators, one of seven feet, one of four, and one of two feet.

April 20th, '82.—This afternoon a Captain, Subaltern, and twenty-four rank and file, (Refugees,) deserted from John's Island, and came to Head Quarters, all armed.

April 21st, '82.—This morning Lieut. Cunningham and self rode to Head Quarters, with a determination to resign our commissions, which were accepted of by Genl. Greene, after making a small pause of half an hour.

I asked him whether he would be so obliging as to advance us a small sum of money, which he very politely refused, and made answer that he had not any money for those people who chose to return home at their own will.

22d April, '82.—This day I was very busily employed in getting ready to start for the northward.

23d April, '82.—This morning Capt. Campbell, Capt. Stevenson, Lieut. Cunningham, Lieut. Arthur and self started, and came on to a Mr. Dunklin's, 28 miles from camp.

24th April.—This day we passed a number of hills, &c., and quartered at Capt. Hail's, 28 miles.

25th April.—Dined at Col. Thompson's. Crossed the Congaree, and quartered at Mr. Dawson's, where we were treated very politely. 26 miles.